ESTHER

For Such a Time as This

DR. DAVID JEREMIAH

P.O. Box 3838
San Diego, CA 92163

Unless otherwise indicated, Scripture verses quoted are taken from the NEW KING JAMES VERSION.

All websites listed herein are accurate at the time of publication but may change in the future or cease to exist. The listing of website references and resources does not imply endorsement of the site's entire contents.

Printed in the United States of America.

CONTENTS

About Dr. David Jeremiah and Turning Point

Dr. David Jeremiah is the founder of Turning Point, a ministry committed to providing Christians with sound Bible teaching relevant to today's changing times through radio and television broadcasts, audio series, books, and live events. Dr. Jeremiah's common-sense teaching on topics such as family, prayer, worship, angels, and biblical prophecy forms the foundation of Turning Point.

David and his wife, Donna, reside in El Cajon, California, where he serves as the senior pastor of Shadow Mountain Community Church. David and Donna have four children and twelve grandchildren.

In 1982, Dr. Jeremiah brought the same solid teaching to San Diego television that he shares weekly with his congregation. Shortly thereafter, Turning Point expanded its ministry to radio. Dr. Jeremiah's inspiring messages can now be heard worldwide on radio, television, and the Internet.

Because Dr. Jeremiah desires to know his listening audience, he travels nationwide holding ministry rallies that touch the hearts and lives of many people. According to Dr. Jeremiah, "At some point in time, everyone reaches a turning point; and for every person, that moment is unique, an experience to hold onto forever. There's so much changing in today's world that sometimes it's difficult to choose the right path. Turning Point offers people an understanding of God's Word as well as the opportunity to make a difference in their lives."

Dr. Jeremiah has authored numerous books, including ***Escape the Coming Night*** (Revelation), ***The Handwriting on the Wall*** (Daniel), ***Overcoming Loneliness, Grand Parenting, The Joy of Encouragement, Prayer—The Great Adventure, God in You*** (Holy Spirit), ***When Your World Falls Apart, Slaying the Giants in Your Life, My Heart's Desire, 31 Days to Happiness—Searching for Heaven on Earth, Captured by Grace, Grace Givers, Signs of Life, What in the World Is Going On? God Loves You: He Always Has—He Always Will, What Are You Afraid Of?, Overcomer, Forward,*** and ***Where Do We Go From Here?.***

How to Use This Study Guide

The purpose of this Turning Point study guide is to reinforce Dr. David Jeremiah's dynamic, in-depth teaching and to aid the reader in applying biblical truth to his or her daily life. This study guide is designed to be used in conjunction with Dr. Jeremiah's *Esther—For Such a Time as This* audio series, but it may also be used by itself for personal or group study.

Structure of the Lessons

Each lesson is based on one of the messages in the *Esther—For Such a Time as This* compact disc series and focuses on specific passages in the Bible. Each lesson is composed of the following elements:

• *Outline*

The outline at the beginning of the lesson gives a clear, concise picture of the topic being studied and provides a helpful framework for readers as they listen to Dr. Jeremiah's teaching.

• *Overview*

The overview summarizes Dr. Jeremiah's teaching on the passage being studied in the lesson. Readers should refer to the Scripture passages in their own Bibles as they study the overview. Unless otherwise indicated, Scripture verses quoted are taken from the New King James Version.

• *Personal and Group Application Questions*

This section contains a variety of questions designed to help readers dig deeper into the lesson and the Scriptures and to apply the lesson to their daily lives. For Bible study groups or Sunday school classes, these questions will provide a springboard for group discussion and interaction.

• *Did You Know?*

This section presents a fascinating fact, historical note, or insight that adds a point of interest to the preceding lesson.

Personal Study

Thank you for selecting *Esther—For Such a Time as This* for your current study. The lessons in this study guide were created to help you gain fresh insights into God's Word and develop new perspectives on topics you may have previously studied. Each lesson is designed to challenge your thinking, and help you grow in your knowledge of Christ. During your study, it is our prayer that you will discover how biblical truth affects every aspect of your life and your relationship with Christ will be strengthened.

When you commit to completing this study guide, try to set apart a time, daily or weekly, to read through the lessons without distraction. Have your Bible nearby when you read the study guide, so you're ready to look up verses if you need to. If you want to use a notebook to write down your thoughts, be sure to have that handy as well. Take your time to think through and answer the questions. If you plan on reading the study guide with a small group, be sure to read ahead and be prepared to take part in the weekly discussions.

Leader's Guide

Thank you for your commitment to lead a group through *Esther —For Such a Time as This.* Being a leader has its own rewards. You may discover that your walk with the Lord deepens through this experience. Throughout the study guide, your group will explore new topics and review study questions that encourage thought-provoking group discussion.

The lessons in this study guide are suitable for Sunday school classes, small-group studies, elective Bible studies, or home Bible study groups. Each lesson is structured to provoke thought and help you grow in your knowledge and understanding of God. There are multiple components in this section that can help you structure your lessons and discussion time, so make sure you read and consider each one.

Before You Begin

Before you begin each meeting, make sure you and your group are well-versed with the content of the chapter. Every person should have his or her own study guide so they can follow along and write in the study guide if need be. When possible, the study guide should be used with the corresponding compact disc series. You may wish to assign the study guide lesson as homework prior to the meeting of the group and then use the meeting time to listen to the CD and discuss the lesson.

To ensure that everyone has a chance to participate in the discussion, the ideal size for a group is around eight to ten people. If there are more than ten people, try to break up the bigger group into smaller subgroups. Make sure the members are committed to participating each week, as this will help create stability and help you better prepare the structure of the meeting.

At the beginning of the study each week, start the session with a question to challenge group members to think about the issues you will be discussing. The members can answer briefly, but the goal is to have an idea in their mind as you go over the lesson. This allows the group members to become engaged and ready to interact with the group.

After reviewing the lesson, try to initiate a free-flowing discussion. Invite group members to bring questions and insights they may have discovered to the next meeting, especially if they were unsure of the meaning of some parts of the lesson. Be prepared to discuss how biblical truth applies to the world we live in today.

Weekly Preparation

As the group leader, here are a few things you can do to prepare for each meeting:

- Choose whether or not you will play the CD message during your small group session.

  If you decide to play the CD message from Dr. Jeremiah as part of the meeting, you will need to adjust the group time accordingly.

- Make sure you are thoroughly familiar with the material in the lesson.

  Make sure you understand the content of the lesson so you know how to structure group time and you are prepared to lead group discussion.

- Decide, ahead of time, which questions you plan to discuss.

  Depending on how much time you have each week, you may not be able to reflect on every question. Select specific questions which you feel will evoke the best discussion.

- Take prayer requests.

  At the end of your discussion, take prayer requests from your group members and pray for each other.

Structuring the Discussion Time

If you need help in organizing your time when planning your group Bible study, here are two schedules, for sixty minutes and ninety minutes, which can give you a structure for the lesson:

Option 1 (Listen to Audio CD)	**60 Minutes**	**90 Minutes**
Welcome: Members arrive and get settled.	N/A	5 minutes
Getting Started Question: Prepares the group for interacting with one another.	Welcome and Getting Started 5 minutes	15 minutes
Message: Listen to the audio CD.	40 minutes	40 minutes
Discussion: Discuss group study questions.	10 minutes	25 minutes
Prayer and Application: Final application for the week and prayer before dismissal.	5 minutes	5 minutes

Option 2 (No Audio CD)	**60 Minutes**	**90 Minutes**
Welcome: Members arrive and get settled.	5 minutes	10 minutes
Getting Started Question: Prepares the group for interacting with one another.	10 minutes	10 minutes
Message: Review the lesson.	15 minutes	25 minutes
Discussion: Discuss group study questions.	25 minutes	35 minutes
Prayer and Application: Final application for the week and prayer before dismissal.	5 minutes	10 minutes

As the group leader, it is up to you to keep track of the time and keep things moving along according to your schedule. If your group is having a good discussion, don't feel the need to stop and move on to the next question. Remember, the purpose is to pull together ideas, and share unique insights on the lesson. Make time each week to discuss how to apply these truths to living for Christ today.

The purpose of discussion is for everyone to participate, but don't be concerned if certain group members are more quiet—they may be internally reflecting on the questions and need time to process their ideas before they can share them.

Group Dynamics

Leading a group study can be a rewarding experience for you and your group members—but that doesn't mean there won't be challenges. Certain members may feel uncomfortable discussing topics that they consider very personal, and might be afraid of being called on. Some members might have disagreements on specific issues. To help prevent these scenarios, consider the following ground rules:

- If someone has a question that may seem off topic, suggest that it is discussed at another time, or ask the group if they are okay with addressing that topic.
- If someone asks a question you don't know the answer to, confess that you don't know and move on. If you feel comfortable, invite other group members to give their opinions, or share their comments based on personal experience.
- If you feel like a couple of people are talking much more than others, direct questions to people who may not have shared yet. You could even ask the more dominating members to help draw out the quiet ones.
- When there is a disagreement, encourage the group members to process the matter in love. Invite members from opposing sides to evaluate their opinions and consider the ideas of the other members. Lead the group through Scripture that addresses the topic, and look for common ground.

When issues arise, remind your group to think of Scripture: "Love one another" (John 13:34), "If it is possible, as much as depends on you, live peaceably with all men" (Romans 12:18), and "Be quick to listen, slow to speak and slow to become angry" (James 1:19, NIV).

For Continuing Study

For a complete listing of Dr. Jeremiah's materials for personal and group study call 1-800-947-1993, go online to www.DavidJeremiah.org, or write to Turning Point, P.O. Box 3838, San Diego, CA 92163.

Dr. Jeremiah's *Turning Point* program is currently heard or viewed around the world on radio, television, and the Internet in English. *Momento Decisivo*, the Spanish translation of Dr. Jeremiah's messages, can be heard on radio in every Spanish speaking country in the world. The television broadcast is also broadcast by satellite throughout the Middle East with Arabic subtitles.

Contact Turning Point for radio and television program times and stations in your area, or visit our website at www.DavidJeremiah.org/stationlocator.

The Book of Esther

INTRODUCTION

Welcome to one of the most beautiful stories of God's sovereignty in the Bible—the book of Esther. In this short Old Testament book, which never once refers to the name of God, His hand can be seen moving in the lives of believers and non-believers alike to bring about His chosen ends.

This study will help you understand why Esther is such an important book, both in the context of history and in the course of our lives. You'll learn just how Esther came to be in the right place at the right time to save an entire nation of Jews from extermination. You'll see how "coincidental" events all worked together to bring an improbable end to Haman, the most powerful national leader and anti-Semite in the Persian Kingdom. And your spirit will be relieved in these days of so much sin and evil to see how God uses even pagan practices and people to accomplish godly goals.

Esther's place as a powerful queen in Persia was set up while she was still an orphan girl being cared for by her cousin and father figure, Mordecai. Mordecai, a Jewish man, was most likely a judge in Persia and held counsel at the gates of the palace.

King Ahasuerus, or Xerxes I (his given name), was desperate to secure his position as a powerful leader who would be able to lead his kingdom into war against Greece. So when his queen, Vashti, refused to appear at his drunken public request, he swiftly banished her from his kingdom. After all, he reasoned, if a king cannot rule his own wife, how will others think he can rule the kingdom?

Xerxes lost the war against Greece anyway and returned home to face defeat and a home without a queen. Thus began a nationwide search for a new woman to wear the crown. All the desirable young women were gathered to await their turn to "audition" for the king and the queenly crown. That is where Esther enters the picture.

Following Mordecai's wise counsel, Esther kept quiet about her Jewish roots and eventually became Xerxes' new queen. There would soon come a day, however, when she would confess her heritage and use her royal privileges to save the Jews from a terrible fate concocted by Xerxes' own friend and chief counselor, Haman.

By all accounts, Haman's biggest problem was pride. He held himself in such high regard that all the people in the kingdom had to bow down at his passing. In this study you'll learn how one man's refusal to bow led to a civil war between the Jews and their enemies within the kingdom. You'll also read of how Haman's pride led to a big downfall.

Each lesson focuses on a small portion of Esther to help you digest all the facts and discern the instructions profitable for your own life. You'll learn about a portion of Jewish history that is related nowhere else in the Bible. You'll find yourself examining your heart closely as you read of the fortunes and misfortunes of the characters in Esther.

God honored those who faithfully stood up for his people, elevating Esther to queen and Mordecai to second-in-command to the king. In this study we hope you'll commit anew to be on God's side, actively seeking His will and spreading His Word, no matter the difficulties. The heavenly rewards are always innumerable.

A Regal Dinner and a Royal Divorce

Esther 1:1-22

In this lesson we will learn about the initial circumstances that enabled Esther to be in the right place to help God's people.

OUTLINE

As we study the beginning of the story of Esther, we will discover that God is in sovereign control and that He leads us even when we are not aware of it.

I. A Regal Dinner
   A. The Intention of the Dinner
   B. The Indulgence of the Dinner

II. A Royal Divorce
   A. The Insubordinate Queen
   B. The Infuriated King
   C. The Impulsive Decree

OVERVIEW

Someone has said that if Adolf Hitler had read and studied and followed the book of Esther instead of *Mein Kampf*, the entire course of history would have been changed. This is the importance of this little book.

In many ways, the book of Esther is one of the most remarkable books in the Bible. The name of God is not mentioned in this book even one time. There is not a divine title or a pronoun that refers to God in any of the chapters of this book.

The book of Esther is also unique in that prayer is not mentioned one time in the book. By establishing the first remarkable thing, we shouldn't be surprised by the second one. If God isn't mentioned, then obviously it wouldn't make much sense to mention prayer either.

The book is also remarkable because it is never quoted in the New Testament. There is not even a casual reference to it. Finally, the book is unusual because it is named for a woman. The only other book in the Bible named for a woman is the book of Ruth.

The setting for the book of Esther is in that land known today as Iran. Before March of 1935, Iran was known as Persia. Persia is a very important country in biblical history.

In the book of Daniel there is an outline of world history. That outline is presented in terms of a great colossus that Daniel viewed, showing a head of gold and arms of silver. It expressed the chronological sequence of the kingdoms of the world. The head of gold represented Babylon, which was ruled then by Nebuchadnezzar. The arms and breast of silver were significant because they represented the kingdom that would ultimately take Babylon away. That kingdom was comprised of the Medes and the Persians.

The Persian Kingdom is stated in Daniel to be inferior to Babylon. Many have labored over what that means, but apparently "inferior" doesn't mean that it was a lesser kingdom in terms of wealth, but in terms of its control.

When Nebuchadnezzar was king over Babylon, he was an absolute monarch. His was the only vote that counted. This is reminiscent of one who tried to succeed him in modern times. Saddam Hussein fancied himself to be a modern Nebuchadnezzar. He was rebuilding the hanging gardens of Babylon for his own pleasure; and on the walls of the new Babylon, he had Nebuchadnezzar's name emblazoned right next to his own. He had pictures taken of himself in a chariot similar to the one Nebuchadnezzar used. Saddam Hussein was the same kind of absolute dictator that Nebuchadnezzar was.

But in the Persian government, the king did not simply dictate. His decisions weren't made that easily. In the book of Esther, the king talks to all of his friends before he decides to do anything. That is the reason Persia is spoken of in Daniel as an inferior kingdom.

The book of Esther is important because it opens up a whole area of Jewish history we would otherwise know nothing about. King Nebuchadnezzar came to Jerusalem and took Daniel and his friends away to Babylon. Ultimately the whole nation was taken captive and remained in captivity for seventy years. The books of Ezra, Nehemiah, Malachi, and other Old Testament prophets record what happened when a small number of those captives returned to Jerusalem. For instance, under Ezra and Nehemiah, some fifty thousand people returned to rebuild the temple and the walls.

But what happened to all the rest of them? By the time the captivity had ended, many of the Jewish people who were in Persia didn't want to go back to Jerusalem. They had become comfortable with the Babylonian lifestyle. Some believed the trouble they got into by staying behind in Persia was due to the fact that their hearts were hardened and they did not return as God told them they should at the end of captivity. Perhaps a lot of the things that happened to them even in the book of Esther were the result of the disobedience.

During the time this book was written, a man named Haman tried to destroy all of the Jews who were left in Persia under King Xerxes. The book of Esther tells us how the Jewish nation was rescued from extermination.

The book of Esther is also important because it explains one of the Jewish feasts practiced even to this day—the Feast of Purim. It was developed by the Jewish people because of what happened to them in the book of Esther. The book explains the origin of this feast, one of the Jewish nation's most festive holidays. The word *îpurimï* means "lots." It refers to the casting of lots by Haman to determine the day on which the Jews would be slaughtered. Today the Jews celebrate the fact that he couldn't pull it off.

God raised up Esther and planted her in Persia under King Xerxes where there was a man by the name of Haman who wanted to obliterate her people. God used that woman significantly to save the people of God from being annihilated, and she was faithful to the challenge God laid before her.

A Regal Dinner

The first chapter of Esther is preliminary to the actual story. It explains how Esther got involved in government in the first place. If you divide the chapter in half, verses 1 through 12 describe the regal dinner. Verses 13 through 22 talk about the royal divorce.

The chapter begins talking about Ahasuerus, which is not the king's name, but a title. It means "high father" or "venerable king." In Rome the leader was the Caesar. In Egypt the leader was the Pharaoh. In Persia the leader was the Ahasuerus. Those who have studied history believe that his real name was Xerxes I.

The Intention of the Dinner

The regal dinner described in the first four verses was for the purpose of bringing together again Ahasuerus' chiefs and leaders who were closest to him for the purpose of going to war against the Greeks. This gathering lasted for 180 days, and at the end of the banquet there was a banquet that ended all banquets.

The Indulgence of the Dinner

This feast lasted seven days and was held in the king's beautiful garden. This gala gathering revealed the wealth, the luxury, and the regal character of this court. The reason for this lavish affair is clear: King Xerxes wanted to win wholehearted support for his military campaign to capture Greece and make himself the supreme ruler of the world of that day. He wanted to show his friends that he had enough money to fund the war. So he brought out all the great treasures of his kingdom including "golden vessels, each vessel being different from the other" (verse 7). These vessels were filled with "royal wine in abundance." Every guest was allowed to drink as much wine as he wanted.

A Royal Divorce

If you read the story carefully, you see that there are two parties going on at the same time. In that particular culture it was not proper for women and men to drink together. Queen Vashti held her own bash for the women.

After all the men were drunk, Xerxes decided he wanted the men to see how beautiful his wife the queen was. So he sent his servants over to get Queen Vashti and bring her back so all of the drunken men could ogle her.

The Insubordinate Queen

Vashti said, "I'm not going!" She had probably sorted the whole thing out in her mind and knew the men were well under the influence of alcohol. She knew that if she went she would place herself in a very poor position. She also knew the law of the land—it was not proper for an unveiled woman to be in the presence of men, and she was trying to keep the law as she understood it. It was the custom for women to be heavily veiled, but she would have to appear unveiled in order for the king to show all of his friends her beauty. She refused to come at the king's command.

The Infuriated King

Imagine that the king has just said to his guests, "I have a real surprise for you. I want you to see my queen. She is going to stand before you with the royal crown upon her head, and I want to tell you, she is a beauty. She'll be here in just a few moments."

Then the chamberlain comes in and whispers in the king's ear, "She won't come."

The king is now embarrassed. He has to turn around and say, "I'm very sorry, gentlemen, but our main attraction is not feeling well tonight. She won't be here."

And the buzzing begins throughout the banquet because everybody knows something is wrong. Remember, they are gathered to decide whether or not they are going to follow the king into war against Greece, and this king cannot even command his own wife.

When you have an insubordinate queen, it isn't long before you have an infuriated king. True to form, the king asked his wise men what they should do to Vashti because she refused to obey his command.

The Impulsive Decree

Evidently there was no law that could force Queen Vashti to obey the king's command to come to the banquet. The cabinet needed to come up with a harsh law to take care of the situation. So Memucan, one of the princes, came forward with a suggestion: "If it gets around the rest of the Persian Kingdom that the queen is not obeying the king, then the rest of the husbands will be despised by their wives also. We need to do something about this." So they enacted the law that banned Vashti and decreed that a wife was to honor her husband and submit to his rule.

This story of Vashti is important because it sets up the situation that brings Esther into the story. After Vashti was divorced and deposed, they decided to run a kind of contest to see who would be the next queen. They brought all of the beautiful women before King Xerxes and chose Esther, placing her in a position of responsibility and authority.

If all of us could write the history of our lives and look back to see how God has led, there would probably be many similar circumstances. God loves to lead us even when we are not aware of His leading. The divorce of Vashti was surely as much a part of God's plan and purpose for Esther as are all the circumstances that follow in this marvelous book. Sometimes when we look at our lives and see things that don't make sense, we wonder what God is up to. But God has a purpose in what He does in the lives of those who love Him. Every thread woven into the fabric of our lives is part of the ultimate tapestry that someday we will view before Him in glory.

Whatever else we may learn from Esther, we will see God's sovereign hand upon His own people and upon the life of this magnificent woman. It all came about because one night a woman didn't listen to her husband when he told her to come to a party. God used that to make a place for Esther.

PERSONAL QUESTIONS

1. Read Esther 1:1-12.

   a. How many months did Ahasuerus (Xerxes) display his wealth?

   b. Who was present at this long gathering?

   c. What material items did the king have at the banquet to give an idea of how wealthy he was?

d. What was Ahasuerus' reason for showing off his wealth?

e. What did the king request of Vashti, his queen?

f. What was the likely reason that Vashti refused his request?

g. How does verse 12 describe Ahasuerus' reaction to her refusal?

2. Read Esther 1:13-22.

    a. Whom did Ahasuerus consult about the situation with Vashti?

    b. What was Memucan's response in verses 16-17?

c. Was Memucan's response a valid concern? Why or why not?

d. What decree did the king make against Vashti? (verse 19)

3. God used this situation to make a way for Esther to become queen and eventually save the Jewish people. Looking back on your life, can you pinpoint a situation that seemed upsetting at the time but that God used for good? If so, describe the situation below.

GROUP QUESTIONS

1. Read Esther 1:1-12 as a group.

   a. Why did King Ahasuerus hold a feast in Shushan?

   b. How long did the gathering last and who attended it?

   c. List some items that describe the wealth of King Ahasuerus. (verses 6-7)

d. In verses 10-11 what did King Ahasuerus request of Queen Vashti?

e. Why might Vashti have refused his request?

f. How did Ahasuerus respond to her refusal? (verse 12)

2. Read Esther 1:13-22 together.

   a. What question did the king ask his wise men in verse 15?

   b. Discuss Memucan's response in verses 16-17. Was this wise advice? Why or why not?

   c. What did King Ahasuerus decide to do after consulting with his wise men? (verses 21-22)

3. If comfortable, share with the group a time when God used a confusing or upsetting situation in your life to bring about His plan in your life.

DID YOU KNOW?

King Xerxes ruled over the kingdoms of Persia, Media, and Babylonia for 21 years (486–465 B.C.). His invasion of Greece in 480 B.C. assembled one of the largest ancient armies ever recorded. Leonidas of Sparta, with his famous 300, arrested his progress at the Pass of Thermopylae where Leonidas was killed. The Persian invasion was defeated at Salamis by Themistocles. When Xerxes returned home after this expensive and long invasion, he began the process of looking for a new queen. Ultimately Esther was chosen. She reigned as queen of Persia for thirteen years.

Esther Becomes Queen

Esther 2:1-23

In this lesson we will learn five principles about God's will.

OUTLINE

As we study the story of how Esther is chosen as the new queen, we will become acquainted with the sovereignty of God in matters that seem difficult.

I. **The Reason for the Beauty Contest**
   A. The Demand for a New Queen
   B. The Insertion of Mordecai and Esther
   C. The Introduction of Esther

II. **The Rules of the Beauty Contest**

III. **The Results of the Beauty Contest**

IV. **Application**
   A. God's Will Is Not Isolated to the Church or to Christians
   B. God's Will Is Not Frustrated by the Failures of Men
   C. God's Will Is Not Negated by Difficult Circumstances
   D. God's Will Is Not Complicated by the Devices of Man
   E. God's Will Is Not Abrogated by Promotions in Life

OVERVIEW

Chapter 2 begins with the words, "After these things," remarking on the circumstances of Queen Vashti being set aside. There is a probability that as many as four years passed between the events at the end of chapter 1 and the beginning of chapter 2. What happened during this time?

Secular history relates that Xerxes carried on his campaign against Greece and was miserably defeated. His entire fleet was destroyed in the Adriatic Sea. When he returned to his summer palace in Shushan, he plunged into excesses of despair. He was an egocentric man who lost a major war upon which he had set his heart. He returned to the palace hoping to find someone who could assuage his grief, but soon realized that he had divorced the one person who had been able to cheer him up in the past—his wife Vashti.

THE REASON FOR THE BEAUTY CONTEST

When the king's assistants realized how sad he was, they insisted a new queen be selected. They knew the laws of the Medes and the Persians could not be countermanded—Queen Vashti could not be brought back. The king had made a decree, and it could not be undone. The only way to restore order to the palace was to conduct a national beauty contest and select a new queen.

The Demand for a New Queen

King Xerxes liked the idea. The search for a new queen extended to the far corners of the empire. The ministers of Ahasuerus suggested the king appoint officers in all the provinces of his kingdom to bring all the fair young virgins to Shushan the palace, and that the young women be placed in the house of women under Hegai, the king's chamberlain. The house of women was where the king's harem was kept.

The Insertion of Mordecai and Esther

In Shushan the palace (or citadel) was a man who came to Babylon before the Persians had taken over the kingdom; he, or his family before him, having been taken there. This man, Mordecai, was probably relatively young during the time this story unfolds.

One of the obvious questions is: Why was Mordecai not back in Israel? The Jews had been under captivity because of their wickedness, but there had come a time when Ezra was allowed to go back and rebuild the walls of the temple. Somewhere between thirty and fifty thousand people were released to go back to Jerusalem. Mordecai had apparently decided that living under the pagan culture of the Babylonians and the Persians was not all that bad. Many Bible scholars believe his presence there at this particular time reflects that he was not in the will of God.

The Introduction of Esther

In verse 7 we are told that Mordecai "had brought up Hadassah, that is, Esther, his uncle's daughter, for she had neither father nor mother. The young woman was lovely and beautiful. When her father and mother died, Mordecai took her as his own daughter."

Hadassah's other name, Esther, was probably given to her by her captives. Most scholars believe the name Esther was originally related to a Babylonian deity named Ishtar, connected with the fertility cult of mother and child. The name *Hadassah* means "myrtle."

Esther was brought to the king's house and made a part of the beauty pageant. The Bible does not tell us whether she came willingly or was brought against her will. She was placed in the custody of Hegai "and she obtained his favor; so he readily gave beauty preparations to her, besides her allowance. Then seven choice maidservants were provided for her from the king's palace, and he moved her and her maidservants to the best place in the house of the women" (verse 9). The preferential treatment is not surprising because God was working this out behind the scenes. It was part of His divine plan.

From now on, Esther would be supported by the king. The seven maidens given to her were appointed to attend her in rotation, one for every day of the week. As a mark of the high esteem the keeper of the women had for Esther, he provided special quarters for Esther, which became hers alone. Here again is evidence of God's provision for Esther while she awaited the events that would unfold.

Verse 10 says that during this time, Esther was purposefully secretive about her Jewish identity. Mordecai told her not to talk about it, perhaps to protect her from violence. The Persians may have had an aversion to the Jewish people. Her special treatment may also have provoked a great deal of jealousy among the others being auditioned for queen. (There may have been as many as four hundred women in the contest.)

Some have said that keeping her Jewish identity a secret was tantamount to her rejection and denial of her religion. But it seems obvious that if she had told them who she was, the contest would have been over before it started. God knew what He was doing, and He allowed it to happen.

In verse 11 there is an interesting sidelight about the loving person who had watched over her since she was a tiny girl: "And every day Mordecai paced in front of the court of the women's quarters, to learn of Esther's welfare and what was happening to her." Mordecai was no longer able to care for her needs, but he could not go for a day without thinking of her and wondering how she was doing.

The Rules of the Beauty Contest

The women who were entered in this contest had an entire year of preparation before their moment with the king. These months of purification were for the beautification practices of the day. They were given twelve months to go to beauty school, to learn how to sharpen all of their charms, and to learn how to make themselves as seductive and charming as possible so they would have the best possible opportunity to attract the king's attention.

Six months were spent with oil of myrrh. Myrrh served a double purpose, being not only fragrant but also credited with purifying powers. In addition to the myrrh there were also sweet odors and other things for the purification of women.

Knowing something of the sensuality and lust of King Xerxes, it is possible that some of these virgins would provide themselves with an aphrodisiac to arouse his passions even more. So much was at stake. Each virgin was given one time where she apparently spent the night with the king. If the king delighted in her, he might ask for her again. But if not, she was no longer part of the contest. If the virgin failed to delight the king, "she would not go in to the king again" (verse 14).

If Esther was a godly woman, as we believe she was, she must have been questioning what she would do when the time came for her to present herself to the king. When the women of the house went to spend their night with the king, they could ask the keeper of the women for anything in the house, such as perfume, to take with them to please the king and attract his attention. But when Esther went, she didn't take anything except what was mandated. She just went. She went knowing that God was with her, knowing that she did not need to add to what the Lord had already provided. She went in her own strength and in the power of the Lord who went with her.

The Results of the Beauty Contest

Verse 17 tells us that after she was taken to King Xerxes, "the king loved Esther more than all the other women, and she obtained grace and favor in his sight more than all the virgins; so he set the royal crown upon her head and made her queen instead of Vashti." The king was so overwhelmed that he decided to throw a great party and give out gifts.

Esther had now been moved out of obscurity into the status of royalty—she was queen. The party had been thrown. She had been established. All of the other women had been dismissed. But even as queen, she kept her identity as a Jewess from her own husband. The reason for that was because Mordecai, the one who had brought her up, told her not to tell him yet. Even though she was the queen, she still had allegiance to the one who had been her overseer in her early days.

Application

There are some very important principles found in this story concerning the will of God that we should remember and apply to our lives.

God's Will Is Not Isolated to the Church or to Christians

One of the overwhelming things in this story is that up to this point, all the orchestration of the will of God involved people in the pagan world. He has been moving people around in His plan who don't even know Him. Xerxes would not have known the Lord. And yet God was at work in his life so that all things would work together for good to those who are called according to the purposes of the Lord.

God's Will Is Not Frustrated by the Failures of Men

If God's will stopped the moment we failed, it would be nonexistent about 98 percent of the time. Look at the story.

Xerxes divorced his wife. That wasn't right. That shouldn't have happened. He carried on one-night stands with a large number of women while choosing the new queen. That wasn't right or godly. But though that isn't part of the directive will of God, it is included as a part of God's will because He uses the wrath of people to praise Him. Sometimes when things go wrong in our lives, we're ready to say it's all over. But God is a master of taking things that look like they are the broken pieces of a life and putting those pieces together in a different order and still bringing glory to His Name in spite of our failures.

God's Will Is Not Negated by Difficult Circumstances

"Esther also was taken to the king's palace" (verse 8). I don't believe she really wanted to go. That was difficult. She grew up without a mother or a father. They had died. That was difficult. But God's will is not negated by the difficult circumstances in our lives.

God's Will Is Not Complicated by the Devices of Man

Esther didn't take any of the things from the house with her. She went in her own strength and the power of the Lord. We don't need to complicate the will of God by assisting Him to accomplish His will. God doesn't need a little nudge from us.

God's Will Is Not Abrogated by Promotions in Life

We can never arrive at a level in life where the will of God doesn't matter anymore. Esther was promoted to queen. She was the number one woman in the kingdom. And yet she still cared what her earthly "father" thought and did what he wanted her to do. What a perfect picture of being submissive to the will of God no matter the circumstances. Esther is a book that will not let us ever forget that God's will is at work in our lives even when we don't know it, even when we try to work against it, even when we resist and deny it. God is at work in our lives if we call ourselves His children.

PERSONAL QUESTIONS

1. What does history tell us about what occurs between chapter 1 and chapter 2 of Esther?

2. Read Esther 2:1-18.

   a. What was the plan for finding a new queen? (verses 2-4)

   b. List the facts we learn about Mordecai in verses 5-7.

   c. Why had Mordecai raised Esther? (verse 7)

d. How is Esther described in verse 7?

e. After Esther was taken to the palace, how was she treated by Hegai? (verse 9)

f. What did Mordecai tell Esther not to tell anyone? (verse 10) Why might Mordecai have told her this?

g. How long did the women have to prepare themselves before they went before the king?

h. What did they do during this time?

i. What occurred when Esther went before the king? (verses 17-18)

3. Read Esther 2:19-23.

   a. What plot did Mordecai uncover in these verses?

   b. Explain why the phrase, "and it was written in the book of the chronicles on the presence of the king" (verse 23), is important.

4. Describe some of the ways that Esther relied on God during this time in her life. How have new situations forced you to rely on God?

GROUP QUESTIONS

1. Read Esther 2:5-7 together.

   a. Discuss why you think Mordecai did not return to Jerusalem with the other captives.

   b. Do you believe that God uses our disobedience as part of His plan? If comfortable, share with the group a time in your life when God used your disobedience to continue His will.

2. Read Esther 2:1-4, 8-18 as a group.

   a. Describe how the beauty pageant for a new queen was organized.

b. What did the women do during the twelve months of preparation?

c. How was Esther treated during this time?

d. What was the end result of the pageant?

3. List and discuss the five applications given in the lesson.

•

•

•

•

•

a. What do these principles teach about the character of God?

b. How does it comfort you to know that God is at work in your life, even when you don't know it and even when you don't understand what is happening?

DID YOU KNOW?

According to 2 Chronicles 36, there were three different deportations of Jews under Nebuchadnezzar. The first came in the days of King Jehoiakim, the second in the days of King Jehoiachin, and the third in the days of a king named Zedekiah. The Jeconiah referred to in Esther 2 is the same referred to as Jehoiachin who was carried away captive in 795 B.C.

Haman's Conspiracy

Esther 3:1-15

In this lesson we will learn about Haman's plan to exterminate the Jews.

OUTLINE

As we study the conspiracy of Haman, we will learn about reasons and results of prejudice and the promise that God gives His people about those who try to harm them.

I. The Prejudice of Haman
- A. The Reason for His Prejudice
- B. The Results of His Prejudice

II. The Plot to Kill the Jews

III. The Permission to Destroy the Jews
- A. Haman Is Given Authority to Act
- B. Haman Is Given Approval to Steal

IV. The Proclamation of the Plan
- A. The Plan Documented
- B. The Plan Delivered

OVERVIEW

At the end of the year of Adolf Hitler's greatest triumphs, he boasted, "God, up to now, has placed the stamp of approval on our battle. The year 1941 will bring completion of the greatest victory of our history." Hitler didn't know that God had spoken to Abraham some words to make Hitler's victory impossible. God had said, "I will make you a great nation. I will bless those who bless you, and I will curse him who curses you" (Genesis 12:1-3). God was speaking to the Jewish nation that Hitler had put out his hand to destroy. In doing so, the Nazi leader doomed himself. Within a few short years, Hitler and his military might were destroyed.

Hitler is perhaps the most famous among many who set out to destroy God's people. The enemies of the Jews have made themselves infamous because they sought to annihilate the people of God. One of these is spoken of in the third chapter of Esther. His name is Haman.

The Prejudice of Haman

Haman was promoted in Persia by King Xerxes to a position that would probably correspond to that of prime minister. He was above all of the others in the king's cabinet. All who passed by this man were required to do reverence and bow down.

Today he is the most scorned and hated of men to the Jews. His title is Haman the son of Hammedatha the Agagite, the Jew's enemy. When his name is mentioned even now, orthodox Jews spit and curse him, so hateful is his memory.

The Reason for His Prejudice

Why was Haman so prejudiced against the Jews? Haman was an Agagite. He was from the lineage of the Amalekites who were hated enemies of the Jews. The tradition of the Amalekites was probably as strong as the Jewish tradition. The word had come down to Haman that Saul had destroyed all of the Amalekites and Samuel had hewn in pieces their King Agag. That is probably the reason for Haman's hatred and his prejudice against the Jews.

The Results of His Prejudice

We don't know much of Haman's background, but we do know that he showed a ridiculous need for appreciation. He insisted that people bow down to him. Apparently of all those who were required to do it, there was only one who wouldn't. That one drove Haman crazy. He could have continued as prime minister to the king of Persia if he had been content to let that one man go. But he couldn't do it. He was obsessed and willing to risk everything in order to punish the one person who had refused to bow down before him.

Haman was told by the king's servants that Mordecai was a Jew. And Haman realized that since Mordecai was a Jew, perhaps this was his opportunity to vent his wrath on all of the Jews. He would not get just Mordecai in this plot, but all of the Jews in Persia. That was his goal. Haman's action was the first recorded effort to exterminate the Jews in the Bible.

Pharaoh tried to limit their numbers by ordering the massacre of male babies, but he never tried to exterminate the whole race. Various tribes in Cana resisted the Jewish invasion, and Nebuchadnezzar carried the nation away into captivity, but until this place in the Bible there was no attempt on the part of anyone to exterminate the whole Jewish race. The word "destroy" in verse 6 literally means "to wipe out." Haman could easily have rid himself of one unyielding Jew, but he wanted to wipe out the whole race. He was filled with wrath. He equated Mordecai with the whole Jewish nation. Though he could have dealt with Mordecai individually, he chose rather to use Mordecai as the springboard to destroy all the hated Jews.

In his distorted vision, he didn't see the hundreds of humble Jewish artisans and craftsmen. He didn't see the inoffensive women and children. All he saw was one Jew who insulted him, and he indicted an entire race because of one man.

That is what prejudice is like. It exaggerates one person into an entire race. It blows everything out of proportion. It gets more unreasonable as time goes by until a person who is filled with racism and prejudice has lost all sense and rationality completely. Haman was filled with prejudice; and because of that, he constructed a plot to destroy the Jews.

The Plot to Kill the Jews

In the seventh verse we learn that five years have passed since Esther became queen. At this time, Haman paused to learn the most propitious time to wipe out the Jewish nation. It was Nisan, roughly April, which is the first month of the year in the Persian calendar. The Persians believed that in the first of the year their gods would come together to fix the fates of men.

Haman called in the soothsayers and the witches and all the astrologers and the brain trust. They cast stones, painted or carved stones with markings, like dice. Perhaps they used pieces of wood or strips of papyrus or parchment. The experts in Persia cast these lots, or *pur*, for each day of the year to find which would be the luckiest day of the year to exterminate the Jewish race. The word *pur* comes from a primitive root which means "to crush, to break, to bring to naught."

After choosing the day of destruction, Haman went before Xerxes. He didn't say a word about his personal reasons for destroying the Jews. He didn't even mention Mordecai by name or bring any charge against him. He began by saying there was a certain people scattered abroad and dispersed among all the king's provinces. Then Haman moved from fact to fiction. Some of his words were true. The Jews were a different people. They adhered to a certain law. They observed their own special days. They wouldn't give their daughters to other people in marriage. They wouldn't accept other people's daughters in marriage. On some days when people wanted to do business with them, they shut their stores. And the days other people wanted to observe as holidays, the Jews said were lawful days to do business and they kept their doors open. But Haman took all that and moved it into a picture of treason in the Persian Empire. That was a fabrication.

First having communicated this to the king, he then supposed a problem, and then he suggested the motivation for King Xerxes to be involved in the extermination of the Jews. He said he would pay ten thousand talents of silver into the hands of those who carried out the extermination of the Jews, and that the money would come into the king's treasury.

Other than greed, why would King Xerxes have been interested in that? Because he had lost his campaign against Greece, which had depleted his resources. Haman used some monetary motivations to get this king involved in this project of exterminating the Jews. This monetary motivation (ten thousand talents of silver) was about twenty million dollars.

Where would Haman get that kind of money? From the Jewish nation. He would exterminate the Jews and confiscate their goods. He would take their money and their property and turn that into the ransom he had promised the king—with plenty left over for himself.

The Permission to Destroy the Jews

An amazing thing is that Xerxes did not even inquire about the people Haman wanted to exterminate. He didn't know that one of them was his own wife, Esther. Without asking any questions, he just said, "Get on with it and let me help you get the process started."

Haman Is Given Authority to Act

Xerxes handed over his signet ring to Haman, giving Haman power to act in the name of the king. In ancient times, the kings signified things through their signet ring. The signet ring would have a special design in it. It would be placed in soft wax, and the mark that it left would be just like our signatures are today. It was binding in every legal document.

With the king's signet ring, Haman had the authority of the royal decree in his hands. Now he had everything he needed to destroy the Jewish nation.

Haman Is Given Approval to Steal

In verse 11 the king said to Haman, "The money and the people are given to you, to do with them as seems good to you." This money can't be referring to the silver Haman promised to the king, because it had not yet been paid. It is probably a reference to the money of the people he is going to exterminate. In other words, King Xerxes is saying, "The people are yours, and all their goods are yours. Do with them as you please."

Haman is given the motivation to keep anything he can get from the extermination of the Jews. Haman saw the opportunity not only to exterminate them, but also to fill his own pockets with that which they had acquired.

The Proclamation of the Plan

Haman summoned the king's scribes, and they wrote out the order in the language of each province. Haman used this opportunity as a privilege to whip up anti-Semitism throughout the empire. As this process was boiling there in Shushan the palace, the word undoubtedly began to spread concerning the diabolical act that was about to transpire in the land.

The Plan Documented

Those who have studied this fateful document point out how carefully it was written. It is reminiscent of a modern legal document. The objectives are stated in every possible way so that there can be no way to escape on the part of anyone who might dare not to carry out the order. The extermination is described in three different ways: "to destroy, to kill, and to annihilate all the Jews" (verse 13). How many of the Jews? All of them. Both young and old, including little children and women. How long were they given to do it? One day. So carefully orchestrated was this that when it was written in the language of the people, there could be no doubt what was meant to happen to the Jews. It was signed with the king's name and sealed with his signet ring pressed in the wax of every single paper.

The Plan Delivered

The plan was documented, and the copies of the commandment were carefully delivered. Scholars have told us that Haman used the Persian postal system to send the commandment to every province in Persia. Herodotus wrote, "Nothing mortal travels as fast as these Persian messengers. Along the road men were stationed with horses allowing one man and one horse for each day. And these men will not be hindered from accomplishing at their best speed the distance which they have to go either by snow or rain or heat or by the darkness of night." It was an ancient Pony Express.

A message could go to the farthest reaches of the empire in two or three weeks. An ordinary traveler would require three months to cover the same distance. The edict was published to all peoples so that they would be ready for that day. While the news was going out, Xerxes and Haman sat down and had a drink.

There is a story about a Jew who attended one of Hitler's Munich rallies. While Hitler was raving against the Jews, this man distracted him by laughing. Later, when Hitler asked this man who he was and why he was laughing, the man said, "I am a Jew. You're not the first ruler who tried to destroy us. Once Pharaoh wanted us slain, and now every year at Passover, we eat matzoth. Later Haman tried to annihilate us, so now each year we eat the delicious Manataschen. And I couldn't help laughing, wondering what delicacy we will eat to the commemoration of your downfall." That was one Jew who knew the promise of God.

PERSONAL QUESTIONS

1. Read Esther 3:1-15.

   a. Who was Haman and what was his position in the palace? (verse 1)

   b. What were all of the king's servants required to do when Haman walked by? (verse 2)

   c. Why didn't Mordecai obey this command? (verse 4)

d. How did Haman feel about Mordecai's disobedience and what did he seek to do because of it? (verses 5-6)

e. For what reason did Haman cast lots in verse 7?

f. What plan did Haman present to the king? (verses 8-9)

g. Describe the king's response to Haman's plan to destroy the Jewish people. (verses 10-11)

h. How was the decree issued to all of the Persian Empire? (verses 12-15)

2. Explain why Haman was so prejudiced against the Jews.

3. How does Scripture tell us we should act toward people who are different from us? Try to list a specific Bible reference for each thought.

4. List one way you can show love today to someone you don't always get along with.

GROUP QUESTIONS

1. Read Esther 3:1-15 as a group.

   a. Discuss who Haman was and why he was prejudiced against the Jewish people.

   b. Why did he become angry with Mordecai? (verse 5)

   c. How did Haman describe the Jews to King Ahasuerus? (verse 8)

d. What did the decree of the king say? (verse 13)

e. Discuss how the Jews must have felt after this decree was issued.

f. How does the end of verse 15 describe the people of Shushan after they heard the decree? Why might this be?

2. Discuss some of the reasons for prejudice in our current culture.

a. How can we as Christians fight prejudice in our own hearts?

b. What are some of the ways the Bible says we are to treat others? List a specific Scripture verse for each way.

c. As a group, pray for God to give each of you a heart of compassion and love for others, including those whose lives and cultures are different from yours.

DID YOU KNOW?

There may have been as many as 127 different languages in the vast Persian Empire. Haman's order had to be translated into each of these languages. There were hundreds of hours of work involved in translating this decree so that all the people in the Persian Empire could hear it in their own tongue.

If I Perish, I Perish

Esther 4:1-17

In this lesson we will learn about the sovereign hand of God.

OUTLINE

As we study the effects of the edict to destroy all the Jews in the Persian Empire, we will learn that survival isn't the only issue and that we must cooperate with God in whatever situations He places us.

I. **The Distress of a Nation**

II. **The Disgrace of a Queen**

III. **The Direction of a Patriot**

IV. **The Dilemma of the Law**

V. **The Definition of Sovereignty**

VI. **The Decision of a Lifetime**

VII. **Application**

A. God's Sovereignty Explains What Man Alone Can Never Fathom

B. God's Sovereignty Encircles Even Those Who Don't Know Him

C. God's Sovereignty Encourages Us in Difficult Situations

D. God's Sovereignty Exempts No One From Personal Decisions

E. God's Sovereignty Exalts the Importance of Each Individual

OVERVIEW

Just as surely as Esther was in God's plan, Haman was part of the plan of God. God is not surprised by the Hamans in our lives. God knows all about them. He has allowed them within His sovereign will.

The Distress of a Nation

The news of the edict to destroy all the Jews caused Mordecai to go into deep mourning. He went about the streets of Shushan, the palace city, wailing out loud. His garments were torn. Hebrew and Persian alike understood that Mordecai was expressing great grief and discouragement.

The Bible says he put on sackcloth. Sackcloth was a cloth made from the hair of goats and sometimes from the hair of camels. It was very uncomfortable to wear next to the skin. Often in mourning or expressing grief, the Jewish people especially would wear this uncomfortable cloth next to their skin as an irritation to remind them of their sorrow. If they didn't wear it next to their skin, they would put it over their clothes. It was a sign to everyone that they were in deep mourning, often over the death of a loved one or because of some expected national calamity. Mordecai was expressing strong feelings about what was going on in that nation.

Mordecai went before the king's gate, which was a daring move on his part. No one could enter into the king's gate clothed in sackcloth, but he came as close as he could. After parading his grief around the city, Mordecai went to the city square and marched in front of the king's gate. All that he felt in his heart was being expressed outwardly on his body.

In each and every province wherever the king's decree had been published, there was great mourning among the Jews and fasting and weeping and wailing. Many of the Jews like Mordecai lay in sackcloth and ashes to express their sorrows. To the very far reaches of the empire, Jews mourned and fasted.

Every one of the Jews who received a copy of this decree or heard it read publicly knew this same Xerxes had deposed his first wife Vashti and could not bring her back because it was the law of the Medes and the Persians. Once the king had signed the decree, it could never be undone. This was the sentence of death for every one of the Jews, and they knew it.

The Disgrace of a Queen

When Esther heard what Mordecai was doing, she sent him some clothes and tried to get him out of the sackcloth. Some people think she was trying to get Mordecai cleaned up so he could come into the palace and make his presentation before the king. It is more probable that she was embarrassed to have him moaning and wailing in sackcloth. The clothes she gave him were probably nice clothes, the kind you wear if you are connected to the king's house.

Mordecai refused the clothes. He was not going to remove the stigma. He was not going to accept any fancy clothes from his daughter the queen. When the clothes came back to Esther, she knew something serious was going on. It was Mordecai's way of sending a message back to the queen that this was not just a moment of sorrow or a day of mourning but a national calamity.

The Direction of a Patriot

Esther couldn't go outside the gate herself, and Mordecai, because of the way he was dressed, couldn't go inside the gate. Somehow they had to communicate, so a messenger was chosen. Esther must have chosen someone she could trust. Some have felt it might have been one of the eunuchs of the kingdom. This messenger was supposed to go and express the word faithfully without adding to it or taking from it.

Mordecai felt the best way he could convey the seriousness of this event back to Esther was by sending her a written copy of the edict which had gone throughout all the land saying that every Jew had to be destroyed. Mordecai gave a copy of that edict to Hathach, and Hathach took it to Esther with the message that Mordecai wanted her to appeal to the king. Then she read with her own eyes the death sentence that was passed, not just upon the Jews in the kingdom but upon herself as well, for she was a Jew.

The Dilemma of the Law

Esther respectfully sent back a message that she could not go in to the king as Mordecai had asked. There was a law that everyone knew about that if you walked into the presence of the king when you weren't invited, you faced death. The only safe way to come before the king was if an audience was provided for you. There was one very risky option: Boldly go before the king with the hope that he extended his royal scepter to you, which meant you were welcome. Nobody wanted to take that risk because it was either instant acceptance or instant death.

To add to Esther's concern, she didn't seem to be "in" with the king at that time. He hadn't called for her for thirty days. Evidently he was being entertained by some of the other women from his harem. So Esther passed off the responsibility that Mordecai tried to place on her.

The Definition of Sovereignty

Mordecai returned a message, basically saying to her: "Don't think you're going to get free. If this decree is executed, it will be found out that you are a Jewess and you will die with the rest of the Jews." And then he went on to give two other points about their situation.

The first point mentioned previously was that Esther could be killed. The second point was that Esther might be passed over. Mordecai told her that she might be the answer, but she wasn't the only possibility. Some help or deliverance could come for the Jews from some other place. From the human perspective, Esther looked like the Jews' only hope. But obviously Mordecai was a man of faith, and though he didn't see any other option, he may have thought God had another way to come through on behalf of His people.

The third point he made was that Esther might have been born for a time like this. God might have placed Esther right in the center of that situation so that she could be God's person, even though it was a very uncomfortable situation.

The Decision of a Lifetime

Esther responded by asking Mordecai to gather the Jews together and have them fast for three days. She and her maidens would fast also, and then she would go against the law and appear before the king. She ended by saying, "If I perish, I perish!" (verse 16) Her response to the possibility that she may have been born for this time was to say, "If that's true, then I'll do what I should. And if it ends up that I die, so be it."

Perhaps this wasn't a spiritual decision so much as a sorting out of her options. If she was going to die in eleven months anyway, she might as well take the risk and have the possibility of escaping death if God was indeed in this whole thing. But whatever she meant by what she said, her words have come down to us with great power. They are a reminder that the important issue is that we cooperate with God Almighty and that we be available to Him so that He can use us wherever He has placed us in the situations we face.

Application

God's Sovereignty Explains What Man Alone Can Never Fathom

The greatest minds in history have wrestled with the issue of the sovereignty of God versus the free will of humankind. It is one of the most difficult subjects to discuss. Some day in eternity we may discover how the track of God's sovereignty and the track of our responsibility finally come together. But the way we should look at this is so simple we sometimes miss it: Let God take care of His sovereignty and let us take care of our responsibility. God's sovereignty explains things that humans cannot possibly fathom. Some Bible teachers talk about how the sovereignty of God in our lives, from our perspective, is like looking at a weaving from the wrong side. We see all the various threads and knots and strands sticking out. We see it from the back side because we do not have the perspective that God has. But some day in eternity God will take that patchwork we have looked at and haven't understood, and He will turn it around. We will see the beautiful tapestry that has been woven out of our lives. We can spend all our lives trying to figure out why God does this and why God does that. Sometimes we just have to fall back on the fact that God is sovereign and in control. We can rest secure in that.

God's Sovereignty Encircles Even Those Who Don't Know Him

Sometimes we think that God's sovereignty is just for God's people. But sovereignty drew Haman inside of its circle. He is just as much a player on the stage as Mordecai.

The sovereignty of God drew the wicked, pleasure-loving Xerxes into His circle. Later on in the book, eight hundred Jew-haters will be drawn into the sovereignty of God. They don't know it. They don't have any idea that they are players on the stage. But God used them and allowed them to perform as a part of His ultimate plan, just as surely as Mordecai and Esther were in the center of God's purpose.

God doesn't have one world that He operates for the believer and another world that affects all unbelievers. Even those who do not know God are a part of God's sovereignty.

God's Sovereignty Encourages Us in Difficult Situations

Esther did not understand why she was in that very precarious situation. But if she understood the sovereignty of God, she could have found encouragement in that. God puts us in places we don't understand, but if we believe there are no accidents with God and if we are walking in complete obedience to the will of God, no matter what the situation may be, we can take great comfort in knowing that our God who loves us will not allow anything to happen to us outside of His sovereign control. Everything that comes into our lives passes through the hands of our Heavenly Father.

I don't have a God who goes on vacation. I don't have a God who wakes up and wonders what happened. He doesn't say, "Oh my goodness, I forgot about you guys! And look what a mess you've gotten yourselves into." No, God knows. When I realize that, I recognize I can take courage in my own heart.

God's Sovereignty Exempts No One From Personal Decisions

Some people say, "What's the sense of thinking about it? I don't have any decisions to make. God is in control. What will be, will be." Look at the story: Esther had an agonizing decision to make. Would she walk before King Xerxes and risk her life, or not? God didn't just swoop down on her and make her do that. She was left to make that decision. Esther's words, "If I perish, I perish," in verse 16 are filled with the agony of her own personal choice to do what she believed God wanted her to do.

God's Sovereignty Exalts the Importance of Each Individual

Esther, by herself, in the right place at the right time making the right decisions in obedience to God, stemmed the tide that could have ultimately destroyed the entire Jewish nation—which could have sidetracked the redemption of each of us. Jesus came out of the lineage of the Jews. Esther could not have realized when she was made queen what awesome responsibility she would have. Yet she alone, just one somebody, turned the course of world events. The sovereignty of God exalts the importance of just one person because God uses everybody in His plan. He has no throwaways. Nobody is meaningless in the providence of God.

PERSONAL QUESTIONS

1. Read Esther 4:1-3.

   a. What was Mordecai's response to the king's decree?

   b. Explain the significance of sackcloth and ashes to the Jewish people.

2. Read Esther 4:4-17.

   a. How did Esther respond when she heard what Mordecai was doing? (verses 4-5)

b. Whom did Esther trust to communicate with Mordecai on her behalf? (verse 5)

c. What message did Mordecai send to Esther and what did he ask her to do? (verses 7-8)

d. What was Esther's reply to Mordecai's request? (verse 11)

e. Why was Esther hesitant to do as Mordecai asked?

f. In verses 13-14, how did Mordecai communicate the importance of this situation to Esther?

g. How did Esther respond to Mordecai's plea for her to act? (verse 16)

h. What does her response teach you about her character?

3. What have you learned about God's sovereignty while studying the first four chapters of Esther?

GROUP QUESTIONS

1. Read Esther 4:1-2 together.

   a. Discuss Mordecai's response to the kings' decree which was given in chapter 3.

   b. How does this response differ to how people today normally respond to upsetting news?

2. Read Esther 4:4-17 as a group.

   a. Describe how Mordecai and Esther communicated with each other.

   b. How important do you think it was for Esther to have someone she trusted communicate with Mordecai on her behalf?

c. In your own words, write out what Esther's first response to Mordecai was. (verse 11)

d. How did Mordecai respond to her in verses 13-14?

e. What was Esther's final decision in verse 16?

f. How does this decision demonstrate Esther's courage and trust in God?

3. Share with the group any lessons you have learned about God's sovereignty after studying the first four chapters of Esther.

DID YOU KNOW?

In every chapter in the book of Esther, except chapter 4, there is some kind of feasting recorded. The first chapter has the six-month and seven-day feast of the king and the additional feast of the queen. The second chapter records the feast celebrating Esther's elevation to queen. The third chapter holds the parting of Xerxes and Haman after the terrible decree. In every succeeding chapter, feasting holds a prominent place. But in this fourth chapter, there is no feasting. There is only fasting because of the great sorrow in the land from the irreversible decree of death for the Jews.

LESSON 5

Courage in a Crisis

Esther 5:1-14

In this lesson we will see that courage is persevering in spite of fear.

OUTLINE

As we study Esther's interview with the king, we will learn how critical it is to prepare, and that God is still working while we are waiting for that crucial moment to happen.

I. **Esther's Interview**

II. **The King's Invitation**

III. **Haman's Irritation**

IV. **Application**
   A. The More Crucial the Project, the More Critical the Preparation
   B. Often While We Are Waiting, God Is Working
   C. If You Are Waiting on the Important Issues, You Can Still Be Working on the Mundane
   D. When Your Course Is Righteous, Your Courage Will Be Reinforced

OVERVIEW

How do people face the challenges of life without God? The book of Esther teaches us that we can learn how to trust God in such a way that when the moment of crisis comes we can have the courage to be God's person. It may not be a national crisis like the one Esther intervened in. It may be a crisis in your family, in your business. It may be a crisis in your own personal well-being. But if you know the God of Esther, you can face the crisis with courage, and you can win in the end.

Esther's Interview

Esther went in before the king on the third day of her fasting. According to Jewish reckoning, Esther and her maidens fasted part of the first day, the full second day, and part of the third. By implication we can also believe they were praying. They were probably dressed in the clothing of fasting—sackcloth and ashes—as the Jews were prone to do when they were seriously reaching out to God.

On the third day, Esther took off her mourning clothes and put on her queenly garb. She was going to approach the main entrance to the place where King Xerxes sat. She was going to seek an audience with the king. In doing this, Esther knew that she was violating the law and risking her life. If the king for some reason was not in the mood to summon her with the golden scepter, her life would be over, and she knew it.

The scepter moved. Esther walked the length of the long hallway and touched the end of the scepter to complete the process of being accepted before the king in this impromptu visit. And the king said to her, "What do you wish, Queen Esther? What is your request? It shall be given to you—up to half the kingdom!" (verse 3) It is evident in his statement that Xerxes was aware that this was more than just a casual visit from the queen. Nobody could have realized more than Xerxes that Esther had actually risked her life in order to have an audience with him. Only something of great importance would have caused her to do that. The king responded by saying that he wanted to do whatever it was Esther wanted him to do.

The King's Invitation

Esther had decided at that time not to blurt out what she wanted. She was a woman of great restraint. She had a blank check from the king, but she did not tell him what she desired. Instead, she decided to invite the king to a special banquet. She was going to put him in a position where he could not refuse her. She said to the king, "If it pleases the king, let the king and Haman come today to the banquet that I have prepared for him" (verse 4).

Haman had become the king's favorite son. King Xerxes didn't know what Esther's feeling toward Haman was at this time. He was probably very taken by the fact that not only had Esther invited him to this dinner, but she had also invited the man who had been set up to carry out the process of exterminating all the Jews and bringing great treasures into the Persian economy. And she had also already prepared the banquet. Haman and Xerxes need only attend.

Esther understood that the king had a love of high living. He was a banqueting king. She also knew that he valued Haman. So she played right to the king's interest. She put herself in the best possible situation to get her request granted.

The feeling of the king shows in his response. Not only is he ready to give her half of his kingdom, but he orders rather than invites Haman to come. Haman is the prime minister, the favorite son, the recent holder of the signet ring; but when the queen offers a dinner, Haman has no say in it at all. He is ordered to come quickly to the palace and dine with Xerxes and Queen Esther.

Esther, meanwhile, played upon the curiosity of the king. He wanted to know what she wanted, and she told him "Not yet. Why don't you come to dinner with me?" He asked her again at the banquet. Again he offered her up to half of his kingdom. But the irony is that the thing she wanted was the removal of the man who was dining with them.

She began her statement, "My petition and request is this." Some believe that at this moment she meant to make a request. It is almost like the statement is interrupted. Maybe the whisper of God in her heart stopped her. Maybe she looked at the king's face and realized it was not the right moment.

She obviously was not aware of the fact that what she was going to request was not yet fully prepared on the other side of the ledger. In the next 24 hours, Haman would build a gallows for hanging Mordecai and then make his ultimate reach for honor. In those same 24 hours, the virtue of Mordecai would be brought strangely before the king's remembrance. Esther didn't know any of this, but just as she was about to make her request, she seemed to be stopped. And once again she invited the king and Haman to a banquet the next day.

Haman's Irritation

If Xerxes was confused about what was happening, think about what was going on in Haman's mind. He didn't even know why he got invited to the first banquet. Now he had another invitation for the next meeting. Still, he left the banquet happy—he had just had a private dinner with the king and the queen. No other guests had been invited. He had an invitation for the next night. He came out of this great moment and walked down the street. He saw a lowly man by the name of Mordecai. This man was insignificant in the overall scheme of things, considering Haman's great moment. But Mordecai wouldn't stand up and bow before Haman. It drove Haman crazy.

Someone has said you can tell the character of a person by what irritates them. Little people are irritated by little things. Big people don't get irritated except by big things. But Haman was a little person. This insignificant incident of a righteous Jew not bowing down to him infuriated him. So he went home and tried to impress his friends and family because his self-esteem was hurt.

He started to brag. He bragged about his riches, about the number of his children, about what the king had said about him and how he had been promoted and invited to parties by the queen. Haman was full of himself, yet there was one thing that was still burning him. He said, "Yet all this avails me nothing, so long as I see Mordecai the Jew sitting at the king's gate" (verse 13). This man was wealthy; he'd been promoted to the highest level in the land and had private meetings with the king and queen, but all he could see was that someone wouldn't do what he wanted him to do. Mordecai wouldn't bow, and it drove Haman crazy.

His wife and friends had probably heard this speech a thousand times. So they told him to make a gallows for Mordecai to be hanged on so that Haman could go happily on with his life. Haman thought it was a great idea. He didn't have any idea that he was constructing the instrument of his own death. Apparently they built the gallows through the night. Haman went to bed thinking that all was well and his major problem was about to be solved. He was going to get rid of Mordecai. Little did he dream that he was simply carrying out the will of God in preparing for his own execution.

Application

The More Crucial the Project, the More Critical the Preparation

Esther did not go in to her audience with the king without having prepared herself and having used all of the Jewish people throughout the land in her preparation. She had them fast for three days, and she herself fasted for three days. Why did she do that? She did it to prepare for the critical moment.

Sometimes we think the time spent in spiritual preparation is wasted time. When there is no effort that seems to be directly related to the end objective, we wonder if perhaps we are spinning our wheels. But time spent preparing spiritually for the moment when we have to make a crucial decision or face a challenge is not wasted time. It is very valuable time in the accomplishment of God's will.

Often While We Are Waiting, God Is Working

While Esther fasted, King Xerxes was subtly being prepared for that moment when Queen Esther would step out from behind one of the columns in the court and he would extend his scepter to her. While Esther postponed her requests for 24 hours, there was a major event taking place in the lives of Haman and of Mordecai. When she refused to utter her request in the first banquet, God used those 24 hours to bring Mordecai back to the king's attention.

Sometimes while we are waiting, we feel like nothing is happening because we can only see the physical realm. In the spiritual realm, God is working. If He asks us to wait, it is because He has some work to do while we are waiting.

If You Are Waiting on the Important Issues, You Can Still Be Working on the Mundane

Sometimes we think waiting means going into total inactivity. But Esther, while she was waiting and fasting, prepared a banquet. While she was waiting on the important issue, she was working on the mundane things that had to be done.

When Your Course Is Righteous, Your Courage Will Be Reinforced

Esther had the righteous cause. She was to stand before the king and plead for the life of her people. Was she afraid? Undoubtedly. But courage is not the absence of fear. Courage is persevering in spite of the fear. Courage doesn't mean being oblivious to danger. People who wait for all the courage they need before they act will never act. But those who take the first little step in the process of courageous activity will be reinforced by God and given greater strength.

A man named Mallory led three expeditions on Mount Everest. All three expeditions failed, and Mallory and most of his party were killed in the last attempt. At a banquet celebrating those brave people, a survivor spoke to a picture of Mount Everest, the unconquerable giant. "We shall someday defeat you because you can't get any bigger, and we can."

The challenges of life will not get much bigger. But building your faith in God can grow you into a giant able to be courageous in any crisis. We build our faith by doing the things that seem hard to us at the time so that we can gain strength to do the really hard things that come to us in the future.

PERSONAL QUESTIONS

1. Read Esther 5:1-8.

   a. On the third day of fasting, what did Esther do?

   b. How did the king respond to her presence? (verse 2)

   c. What questions did the king ask Esther? (verse 3)

d. What was Esther's request according to verse 4?

e. During the banquet, why might Esther not have told the king what her main request was?

f. What did Esther's request for a second banquet allow time for?

2. Sometimes crises involve knowing what you must do but not wanting to do it. Have you ever found yourself in that situation? If so, what did you finally do?

3. Read Esther 5:9-14.

   a. How did Haman feel after he left the banquet with the king and queen? (verse 9)

   b. What quickly changed his mood? (verse 5)

c. What did Haman tell his wife, Zeresh, and his friends in verses 11-12?

d. What was Zeresh's advice to Haman? (verse 14)

e. What did Haman do after hearing his wife's advice? (verse 14)

f. What do these verses teach us about Haman's character?

GROUP QUESTIONS

1. Read Esther 5:1-8 as a group.

   a. Discuss the interaction between Esther and the king.

   b. Share why you think Esther might have asked the king and Haman to a second banquet, instead of sharing her main request.

   c. If applicable, share with the group a time when the Holy Spirit kept you from saying something in a moment of crisis, anger, or confusion.

2. Discuss times when each of you needed courage in a difficult or frightening situation.

   a. Where did you find the courage you needed?

   b. What kinds of situations require the most courage from you?

   c. Explain how God builds our faith by having us do difficult things.

3. Read Esther 5:9-14 together.

   a. Why did Haman's mood change from "joyful" and glad to "indignation" on his way home from the banquet? (verse 9)

   b. What did Haman's wife, Zeresh, suggest he do in order to be rid of Mordecai? (verse 14)

   c. How did he respond to her suggestion? (verse 14)

   d. If you had to describe Haman's character in a few words, what words would you choose?

DID YOU KNOW?

The gallows that Haman had constructed was 50 cubits high. That is equal to seven-and-a-half stories, or 75 feet tall. The purpose was to take Mordecai and hang him on this enormously tall gallows for all the people to see. His purpose was to make a lesson out of the death of a stubborn, rebellious Jew who showed him no honor. Literally, Haman's pride came before his fall.

DIVINE INSOMNIA

Esther 6:1-14

In this lesson we will see that the proverb is true—pride goes before a fall.

OUTLINE

As we study Haman's descent and Mordecai's ascent, we will learn that God often raises up the humble and puts down the proud.

I. The King's Insomnia

II. The King's Inquiry

III. Haman's Ready Reply

IV. The King's Instruction

V. The King's Intimidation

VI. Application

A. God Often Promotes Those Who Least Anticipate It
B. God Often Uses Those Who Least Deserve It
C. God Often Judges Those Who Least Expect It

OVERVIEW

The action in this chapter begins in the bedroom of the king. We are not told why he has insomnia. We are only told that the king could not sleep. Ecclesiastes 5:12 says,

The sleep of a laboring man is sweet,
Whether he eats little or much;
But the abundance of the rich will not permit him to sleep.

Maybe that is why the king could not sleep that night; he had so much money he was afraid he would lose it. We may think as we hear his story that the king's insomnia is just an incidental part of the record. But it is all part of God's divine plan and plot.

The King's Insomnia

A presumably unimportant thing happens in chapter 6 when Xerxes can't sleep. Evidently when the king couldn't sleep, he had someone read him boring books so that he could doze off. He called one of his servants to fetch the chronicles or the records of the kingdom.

The servant that night turned to a certain place in the history of the kingdom when two of the king's chamberlains tried to kill the king. (See Esther 2:21-23.) Mordecai and Esther had found out about it. Mordecai saved the king's life by reporting the plot to Esther, who told the king in Mordecai's name. He should have been rewarded for it. Kings in that particular time were uneasy because there were all kinds of insurrections and revolutions within the kingdom. Few kings had very long reigns. When the king's life was saved, he should have immediately rewarded the person who warned him because that
was one of the ways kings continued to preserve their stability in the kingship. They were always prepared to care for those who helped to keep them safe. But somehow this had been passed over. As the chronicles about Mordecai's valiant effort to preserve his life were read to the king, he asked, "What honor or dignity has been bestowed on Mordecai for this?" (verse 3) The king's servants told him that nothing had been done. Immediately the king was wide awake. Nothing had been done. What could he do to reward Mordecai?

The King's Inquiry

Next the king asked his servants who was in the court. Haman had just come to the court to suggest that the king hang Mordecai on the gallows that had been made for him that night. The king was already working in God's plan to preserve Mordecai. Haman had no idea what would soon transpire.

The king invited Haman in and asked him, "What shall be done for the man whom the king delights to honor?" (verse 6) If you are proud like Haman, you don't even look past your nose. You know others are talking about you. And that's what Haman thought: "Whom would the king delight to honor more than me?" (verse 6) He swelled up like a toad, thinking the king was going to do for Haman whatever Haman told him to do.

All the action in this particular part of the story focuses on Mordecai. The king couldn't wait until morning to reward him. Haman couldn't wait until morning to get permission to hang him. Neither one knew what was in the mind of the other. Haman thought, "This is my moment to get Mordecai hanged." The king thought, "This is my moment to get Mordecai rewarded."

Haman's Ready Reply

In Haman's ready reply to the king, he had no bashfulness whatsoever. He determined that this was his opportunity to enter into royalty. He wanted to wear not just kingly clothing, but the king's very own clothes. He wanted to ride not a horse like the king's, but the very horse the king rode. He wanted the things delivered to one of the most noble princes so that this prince could array him. And finally, Haman wanted to be paraded around the streets and have proclaimed before him that this is what happens when the king honors you.

Little did Haman dream that such was not to be his honor. He was so blinded by his own pride that he could see no one but himself in that place of honor.

The King's Instruction

King Xerxes thought Haman's idea was good. He told Haman to take the royal clothes and the horse and do those very things to Mordecai the Jew.

Haman must have been ready to choke on his words. He had come up with the plan for himself, and now he had to fulfill it in compliance with the king for the one man he hated more than any other man on the earth. Can you imagine what anguish was in his heart? There was nothing that could have been more displeasing, more disgusting, more distasteful to Haman than to put the royal garments on Mordecai, to put him on the king's horse, and to lead him through the streets proclaiming that the king honors this man. To accord him that honor was absolutely mortifying to Haman.

Instead of leading Mordecai through the streets in honor, Haman had intended to hang him on the gallows. The humiliation of Haman at this point was unspeakable. You can imagine the feeling that he had as he led the horse through the street with Mordecai on top. He was now honoring and proclaiming the man who would not bow to him. The proclamations probably caught in his throat like gravel. "This is the man whom the king has chosen to honor." And he had to say it over and over.

As they marched through the streets, they may have passed by the gallows. You could hardly miss a gallows that was 75 feet high. Everything Haman had planned had been turned upside down. Until this time Haman had been on his way up, and Mordecai had been on his way down. At this time, Mordecai is on his way up, and Haman is on his way down. All this took place apart from any human effort on the part of Mordecai or Esther. God orchestrated it all behind the scenes, set it up, and made it happen.

The King's Intimidation

When the honor was over, Mordecai went again to the king's gate. He was reinstated in his old position. He went back to doing what he had been doing before. Imagine how ridiculous the whole proceeding had appeared to Mordecai. He and his people were doomed to death. In the city he would pass posters proclaiming the day of the Jewish doom as it was set on the calendar. He would see Jews mourning in sackcloth and ashes, and he would see the gallows that Haman had erected for him. Here he was riding on the king's horse, almost as a show of triumph in the midst of all the despair and death.

When the parade was over, Mordecai just went back to the king's gate. He didn't go and demand an apartment in the palace. He didn't ask to be promoted and given an office. He took what the king gave him as a matter of honor, and when the honor was done, he just went back to being who he was. May there be many others who, when they are promoted by God, allow the honor to belong to God and don't become puffed up in their own spirit.

Haman had a much different experience. He couldn't believe what he had just been made to do, leading his enemy through the streets. He probably got ill every time he thought about it. He didn't want anybody to see him. He covered his face. His head covering was probably a veil, which was a mark of mourning in those days. He hoped nobody recognized him on the way home. He ran there, embarrassed. Ironically, after he told his wife and friends what had happened, the king's servants came to take him back to the palace for the second banquet that Esther had prepared. It would be the last meal that Haman ever ate.

Application

God Often Promotes Those Who Least Anticipate It

In this chapter, Haman's fortunes head downward, and Mordecai's fortunes take a swing upward. Their reversal illustrates the principle that God often promotes those who least anticipate it. Jesus put this into words in Luke 14:11. "For whoever exalts himself will be humbled, and he who humbles himself will be exalted."

Many of the people God is using today come from humble backgrounds. Yet God has desired and determined that He is going to put His hand on them and raise them up so He gets all the glory. So many of these people are just humble servants who don't want to be a part of the limelight. They are just God's people. God has exalted them because they have been humble.

Then there are other people who have been trusted with a ministry and have forgotten to whom they belong. They became their own people, and in that process they went down in ignominious defeat. God's plan and purpose of graduation up through the ranks is far different than man's. God loves to lift up the humble. God lifted Mordecai the humble Jew, who wouldn't bow to Haman, who went back to the king's gate after his hero's parade.

God Often Uses Those Who Least Deserve It

Xerxes, a Persian, was a man who had no understanding of Jehovah God, but God used him. He used him by keeping him awake one night and not letting him sleep. This man could command the wealth and labor of an empire, but he couldn't command his own sleep. As he was read the records of the kingdom, God unfolded a plan that came from the insomnia of a pagan king.

Over and over again in the Old Testament, God uses people who don't deserve it, who don't even know they are being used. One of the great questions of the Old Testament is how God could use a nation more wicked than Israel to punish Israel. That shouldn't surprise us. God used a donkey on one occasion to accomplish His purpose. God can use anything He chooses, and sometimes God uses those who least deserve to be used to accomplish His purpose.

God Often Judges Those Who Least Expect It

Haman thought that day was going to be his day. He had it all planned out. He was prepared for it to be the greatest day of his life. Everything he wanted, from hanging Mordecai to being exalted, seemed to be happening. And then suddenly the person who thought he lived above the judgment of God found the sword at his neck.

It is interesting to compare the conversation that Haman had with his wife and friends at the end of chapter 5 to the conversation they had in chapter 6. They were suddenly singing a different tune. When Haman was puffed up with the banquet, they said, "You're in charge. Kill the Jew." When Haman was depressed from the parade, they said, "If you're talking about that Jew, you're finished." These two conversations picture Haman the great victor and Haman the defeated foe. God often judges those who least expect it.

It is overwhelming to view the sovereignty of God in the affairs of humankind. There are times we get discouraged, but if we will meditate on the sovereignty of God, we will be encouraged, knowing that the God we serve is in control. He doesn't make any mistakes. If we are in fellowship with Him, walking in His will, what may seem to be a tragedy to us may just be one of the stepping stones that God is using to accomplish His purpose in our lives and the lives of the people we love.

PERSONAL QUESTIONS

1. Read Esther 6:1-14.

   a. The night after Esther's banquet, what did the king experience? (verse 1)

   b. Because of this, what did the king request? (verse 1)

   c. What was the king's response to the story about Mordecai? (verse 3)

d. What was Haman's answer to the king's question, "What shall be done for the man whom the king delights to honor?" (verses 7-9)

e. Describe why Haman might have thought the king was talking about him and not about someone else.

f. Whom did the king tell Haman to honor in the way he suggested? (verse 10)

g. What did Haman's wife, Zeresh, tell him after he led Mordecai through the city? (verse 13)

2. Explain how Luke 14:11 relates to this chapter of Esther.

3. How does this chapter encourage you to trust God as you observe what is happening in the world today?

GROUP QUESTIONS

1. Read Esther 6:1-14 together.

   a. What was read to the king when he was unable to sleep?

   b. When Haman entered the palace, what did the king ask him? (verse 6)

   c. What was Haman's first thought after he heard the question? (verse 6)

   d. Discuss how Haman might have felt when the king told him that the honor was to be given to Mordecai and not to him.

e. How was Mordecai honored for earlier saving the king's life? (verses 10-11)

f. How did Haman's family and friends respond when they heard what had occurred? (verse 13)

2. List the four applications found in this lesson and discuss them together.

   -
   -
   -
   -

3. Share with the group what this lesson has taught you about pride and God's view of it.

DID YOU KNOW?

In ancient times, the wearing of the kingly garments was a sign of the king's favor and the possibility of putting on some of his power. By suggesting that the favored person be attired in the royal clothes, Haman was probably trying to place himself in a position where he could ultimately take Xerxes' place. He didn't want just the honor of being the friend of the king. He wanted to be the king.

Poetic Justice

Esther 7:1-10

In this lesson we learn the power of one person doing what God has called them to do—and seeing justice meted out by God.

OUTLINE

As we study the circumstances of Esther's second banquet, we will see how much of a difference a solitary person can make. We will also learn that God is in charge of repaying evil.

I. **The Dinner That Saved the Jews**

II. **The Disclosure That Shocked the King**

III. **The Discovery That Sentenced the Enemy**

IV. **The Delay That Sealed the Sentence**

V. **The Decree That Settled the Issue**

VI. **Application**
  A. The Delay of Justice Is Not the Denial of Justice
  B. The Deliverance of One May Be the Doom of Another
  C. The Dedication of One Can Make the Difference for Many

OVERVIEW

When the Auca Indians took the lives of five missionaries, they apparently thought they had stamped out the Gospel forever. But Rachel Saint, the sister of one of the five missionaries, went back and lived with those Indians, teaching them to read and write and ultimately sharing with them the Gospel of Jesus Christ. The irony is evident. The one whose brother was murdered becomes the agent of redemption for the murderers.

THE DINNER THAT SAVED THE JEWS

This final banquet that Esther gave for Haman and Xerxes probably took place in a room overlooking a garden. The garden lay between the harem complex where Esther lived and the king's private apartments. We are not told what time the party took place. It was probably in the afternoon rather than in the evening. So much happened later on that same day, it could hardly have taken place at night. Later on that day, Haman was hanged, and Mordecai was received by the king, all of which would have taken a good deal of time.

Esther probably knew all the events that had transpired between the two banquets. She was in daily communication through her chamberlains with her cousin. She probably came into that second banquet without hesitancy or fear, knowing that God had been working through the night, setting up the events that would prepare the way for her to make her statement.

When she arrived at the banquet, the king once again addressed her, calling her Queen Esther. This gave emphasis to the fact that she was a royal person, not just a subject. He treated her with respect and dignity. Again he asked what she wanted, and again he promised that whatever she wanted, even if it meant giving away half of his kingdom, he would give to her. The Lord seems to have put those words in his mouth to assure Esther that she need not fear to present her petition to the king.

THE DISCLOSURE THAT SHOCKED THE KING

The first shock the king received was something he had not known up until this time, that his queen was herself a Jewess. When she admitted that it was her people who were in danger, she identified herself for the very first time with her people the Jews. Mordecai had told her to keep her identity secret early on in the story. But now she came out and made herself known to the king. The king was now aware that, because of her nationality, the plot that Haman had talked him into would jeopardize the life of the woman he loved, his queen.

With boldness bolstered by her desperation, Esther stated her petition for her own life and the lives of her people. She used some words that were actually written in the decree to destroy the Jews. She said, "We have been sold, my people and I, to be destroyed, to be killed, and to be annihilated" (verse 4). How could the king have forgotten that these were the very words he had caused the scribes to write and had sent out to all the provinces? Esther must have used those words to draw the memory of the king back into the seriousness of this moment. Then she mentioned that if it were anything other than the lives of her people, she would not have asked. She said, "We wouldn't have troubled the king, except this is more than a mere change in social status. This is the very life of our nation." (See verse 4.)

The Jews were sentenced to die. The king now knew that his wife was among those sentenced. You can almost see the anger rising up the neck of the king when he realizes that he has been sucked into a plot that could mean the death of Esther and all of her Jewish nation.

The Discovery That Sentenced the Enemy

"So King Ahasuerus answered and said to Queen Esther, 'Who is he, and where is he, who would dare presume in his heart to do such a thing?'" (verse 5) He couldn't imagine that anybody he knew would be responsible. We don't know whether the king forgot that he was a part of this or whether this was a parade of his innocence when in reality he was just as guilty as Haman. Esther answered his question by saying, "The adversary and enemy is this wicked Haman!" (verse 6) Before she mentioned his name, she used three strong words to describe him. He was the adversary, a term that is also used in the Bible to describe Satan. He was the enemy, one who hated the people of God. And as the wicked one, he was the antithesis of goodness. All of these phrases are used to describe Satan, and Haman was a tool in Satan's hands. The enemy of Esther's people had been identified. And he who could devote a nation to destruction without a twinge of remorse was now filled with distress at the thought that he had been found out.

The Delay That Sealed the Sentence

At this shocking moment, the king rose from the banquet table and walked out into the garden. There are some times when it is better not to say what is in your mind until you've gotten your thoughts together. What a stressful moment this was for the king! He could have said the wrong thing. The king was torn over what he would do. His wife had just told him that his best friend was responsible for a plot not only to kill all the Jewish people, but ultimately to take her life. This had not registered with him before. He walked into the garden to collect his thoughts.

While he was in the garden, Haman realized he had one last opportunity to save himself. Now, the custom of the day when banqueting was to recline rather than to sit in high-backed chairs as in modern times. At banquets people mostly drank wine and ate dessert. They would recline on their couches and linger long at the wine after the meal. So when the king went outside, his queen was reclining on her couch. As soon as the king was out of sight, Haman realized that if he had any sort of chance at all to be saved he needed to petition the queen. Little did he know that this would be his undoing.

Haman went over to the queen and begged her. When the king came back, "Haman had fallen across the couch where Esther was" (verse 8). That doesn't mean he tried to seduce her. Surely he was smarter than that. But it does mean that he went to the foot of the couch where she was reclining and began a custom to embrace her feet and to entreat her to stand in his place and to save his life. In his intensity to try to entreat this woman to save his life, he placed himself in a position that caused the king to say, "Will he also assault the queen while I am in the house?" (verse 8)

There is much divergence of opinion as to whether the king really thought Haman was up to no good or whether he used this to get Haman for his indiscretion. The king had caught Haman in a violation of palace etiquette. As soon as the king uttered the words remarking on this, the servants covered Haman's face. This was a sign that he was doomed to die, even though the king had not pronounced death upon him. When they put the bag over his head, that meant there was no chance for Haman to be saved. His sentence was sealed.

The Decree That Settled the Issue

Harbonah was a chamberlain of the king and one of those sent to fetch Vashti to the king's party. He had also been part of the chamberlains who had gone to bring Haman to the banquet. Maybe as he was fetching Haman, he saw the gallows that had been constructed there on Haman's property. At this moment, when he had the opportunity, he reminded the king that this one who had so violated everything the king stood for could be punished on the gallows prepared for Mordecai. On the gallows prepared by Haman, Haman was to hang because God faithfully saw that justice would be done.

Some have said that Esther was not very merciful at this moment. Some have written that she was not righteous because she could have spared Haman's life and she did not. While her heart might have prompted her to be merciful, logic and prudence restrained her, and she let the man die.

There is a revelation of a great truth in the New Testament: "Do not be deceived, God is not mocked; for whatever a man sows, that he will also reap" (Galatians 6:7). Often what we set out to do to others is reaped back on us in the providence of God. A story in the Bible illustrates that. Daniel spent all night in the lions' den, and they did not touch him. But the people who were responsible for putting him there were thrown in after Daniel was taken out and were torn apart before their bodies hit the floor. That which they attempted to do to God's people was turned back on their own heads. So it was with Haman.

Application

The Delay of Justice Is Not the Denial of Justice

Why does God wait so long to execute His justice? Why did He take so long to take care of Haman? Could He not have thwarted him at the beginning? Yes, but perhaps He waited, as He so often does with us, to give him an opportunity to repent. Though we cannot always see it, God is working behind the scenes. His justice is not lost. God is watching over His own.

The Deliverance of One May Be the Doom of Another

Seldom does human life present before our eyes the picture that is in this text. Haman, who is the favorite prime minister of state, the wealthy, the strong, the noble, is hanged on the gallows. Mordecai, the despised Jew whose life is seriously in jeopardy and likely to end promptly, is promoted to the highest favor and the most influence with the king. The deliverance of one is often the doom of another.

It goes even beyond that. Haman was an Amalekite. Because of the Amalekite's hostility against the Israelites, they were singled out for God's judgment. Was it given to them immediately? No, but it was just as sure. The Lord said to Moses, "I will utterly blot out the remembrance of Amalek from under heaven" (Exodus 17:14). The threat was not carried out at once. But it is interesting to note that Haman the Agagite is the last Amalekite mentioned in the Old Testament. Once he is hanged, you never hear of the Amalekites again. God's people are promoted and preserved, and the Amalekites who tried to destroy them are once and for all put out of sight and off the record.

The Dedication of One Can Make the Difference for Many

It is hard to believe that one person can make a difference in the course of human events. But if you subtract Esther from the Old Testament, there is no Jewish nation, there is no Jesus Christ, there is no Bible, there is no hope for humankind because Esther was the link that preserved the Jewish nation. She was one who consecrated her life to God and did what God wanted her to do. God used Esther to turn the events of the world around. He may choose to use you in a significant way as well. The dedication of one can often make the difference for many.

PERSONAL QUESTIONS

1. Read Esther 7:1-10.

   a. What question did the king ask Esther at the second banquet? (verse 2)

   b. How did Esther respond to the king's question? (verses 3-4)

   c. What was the king's response to Esther's request? (verse 5)

   d. What do you think Haman was thinking as he listened to the conversation between the king and queen? How is he described in the last half of verse 6?

e. Why might the king have gone out to the garden after he heard that Haman was the man who requested the Jews be killed?

f. What did Haman do after the king left for the garden? (verse 7)

g. According to verse 8, what was the king's response to Haman's actions?

h. What caused the wrath of the king to subside in verse 10?

2. How does the lesson title "Poetic Justice" aptly describe what happened to Haman in this chapter?

3. What does this lesson teach you about the justice of God?

4. How does knowing God is just give you peace when you are treated unjustly?

GROUP QUESTIONS

1. Read Esther 7:1-10 as a group.

   a. Discuss the conversation between the King Ahasuerus and Queen Esther at the second banquet. (verses 1-6)

   b. What are some words that might describe how Haman felt as he listened to the conversation? How does verse 6 describe his reaction to the conversation?

   c. How did the king respond at the end of the conversation? (verse 7)

   d. What last attempt did Haman make to spare himself from the king's wrath? (verse 7) How did this backfire on him in verse 8?

e. What happened to Haman as soon as the king came back in from the garden? (verses 8-10)

2. What are some other examples from Scripture of when God delayed His justice?

a. What do these examples, as well as the example of Haman, teach us about God's character?

b. How do these examples give us hope when we are waiting for justice to be done on our behalf or the behalf of others?

DID YOU KNOW?

Lord Byron, the English poet, discovered the law of inevitable consequences in his own life. After he had thrown away his life in immorality, he wrote these words:

The thorns which I have reaped
are of the tree I planted.
They have torn me and I bleed.
I should have known what fruit
would spring from such a seed.

Undoing the Undoable

Esther 8:1-17

In this lesson we will see how God's power can reverse what seems to be irreversible.

OUTLINE

As we study how the Jews were spared by a new decree, we will learn more about God's awesome power and decree of life for the world.

- **I. The Evidence of the Reestablishment of Peace Among the Jews**
- **II. The Request of the Queen on Behalf of the Jews**
- **III. The Order Condemning the Jews**
- **IV. The Release of the Ruling Which Liberates the Jews**
- **V. The Return of God's Joy to the Spirits of the Jews**
- **VI. Application**
  - A. The Power of God to Reverse the Irreversible
  - B. The Power of the Gospel to Overrule the Power of Sin
  - C. The Plan of God to Reach the World

OVERVIEW

Almost everywhere you turn in the Old Testament, there is evidence of God's miraculous deliverance of His people. Think of Moses in the bulrushes. Think of Joseph in Egypt. Think of Elijah on Mount Carmel. God is at work in this book. His miraculous power, even though not always seen, is working behind the scenes preserving His special people, the Jews.

Until the end of the last chapter, things have not looked good for the Jews in the book of Esther. When Haman hated Mordecai, it did not look good for the people of God. When Haman's hatred for Mordecai was transferred to the entire Jewish race, things looked even worse. When Esther had not been before the king for thirty days and had to walk into his presence and beg for her people, it seemed like everything was hanging on edge. When Haman was given the signet ring and told he could make any law he wanted concerning the Jews, it seemed as if the story was at its end. When Mordecai refused to bow down to Haman and infuriated his wrath, it looked like it would only be a short time before the whole Jewish population of Persia would be dead.

But Haman was hanged on the gallows he had prepared for Mordecai. God was at work. How would He save His people from the awful decree?

THE EVIDENCE OF THE REESTABLISHMENT OF PEACE AMONG THE JEWS

On the day Haman died, the king gave Haman's property to Esther. In Persia, anyone who forfeited his life to the state automatically forfeited his estate. We might feel bad for Zeresh, who had lost her husband and her estate, except for the fact that she put Haman up to erecting the gallows in the first place.

Esther had revealed her nationality to the king in chapter 7. Now she was very happy and proud to present Mordecai to King Xerxes as her guardian and cousin. The king already had a soft spot in his heart for Mordecai since Mordecai had saved his life. The relationship that was unfolding before the king must have been intriguing to him. His beautiful queen that he loved was related to this man whom he had come to admire.

King Xerxes then gave Mordecai the responsibility of the kingdom. He took off his ring which he had taken back from Haman and gave it to Mordecai. The ring was the power symbol of the kingdom.

The king gave it to Haman on a whim, took it back, and then gave it to Mordecai. He passed his ring around like it was something he wanted everyone in the kingdom to share. He was not a very responsible ruler. Thankfully for the Jews, the power was now in their hands.

The Request of the Queen on Behalf of the Jews

Even though Haman, the enemy of the Jews, had been killed and taken out of the way, his fateful decree had already been written and circulated throughout Persia. The Jews were still scheduled to die on a certain day that had been designated in the decree. While Esther might be free as the queen, the edict that had been put into place by the devices of Haman was still on the books. The law of the Medes and the Persians could not be revoked. Unless something could be done to countermand it, all of Esther's people would be killed.

So Esther approached her husband and set up her request by saying four things first. She said, "If it pleases the king, and if I have found favor in his sight and the thing seems right to the king and I am pleasing in his eyes" (verse 5). Xerxes probably thought, "This is going to be something really big."

Then Esther asked him to reverse the letters that Haman had sent out to destroy the Jews. She appealed with anguish, "For how can I endure to see the evil that will come to my people? Or how can I endure to see the destruction of my countrymen?" (verse 6)

The Order Condemning the Jews

The king then seemed to encourage Esther. He indicated that he was very favorable toward her and the Jews. He reminded her of what he had done for the Jews by giving Esther the house and life of Haman when Haman sought to lay his hands on the Jews. Although Xerxes was anxious to spare the Jews and let them off the hook of his previous decree, he wasn't allowed to change his mind. So he told Mordecai, "You've got the ring. You write a new decree that will overrule the old decree." He had given his power to another, and the other could change his mind. The king even brought in the scribes and made it possible for Mordecai to use the government for this personal pursuit. So Mordecai wrote the new decree to emancipate the Jews.

Now, the first decree went forth on the thirteenth day of the first month, which is April 17 if you use the chronology which we've referred to in an earlier chapter. Two months and ten days had gone by, giving plenty of time for the Jews to experience the anguish of their impending doom. They felt the pain of wondering when the ax would fall.

The second decree was issued and needed to be sent out. Some have wondered why it seemed to take so long to get this process going. It wasn't something that happened immediately. But it didn't have to happen immediately because there was still enough time left before the decree to kill the Jews would be executed. Within that period of time, Esther and Mordecai had to get the new decree out to all the provinces. Since it was so important, they wanted to make absolutely certain they did it right. They made this new decree of life very similar in wording to the old decree of death.

The Release of the Ruling Which Liberates the Jews

Mordecai wrote in the king's name, sealed it with his ring, and sent the letters out. This decree granted the Jews the right to gather themselves together to stand for their lives. They were given permission to avenge themselves against anyone who would come to attack them. They had advance notice so they could prepare. Until now they had been fugitives. They had known nothing of organizing to avenge themselves. They had thought only of their own lives. Now they were given an offense, an opportunity to retaliate, and a support system within their community.

Some have great difficulty with the fact that Mordecai wrote a decree that the Jewish people could kill even the women and the children. But the verse doesn't say the Jewish people were given *carte blanche* to go out into the community in Persia and find anyone, assault them, kill the babies, and kill the women. No, the decree said that if the Persians came against the Jews, they could defend themselves against their enemies.

The Return of God's Joy to the Spirits of the Jews

The Jews now had what they needed to go out and preserve their nation against attack. It shouldn't come as a surprise that they rejoiced. Mordecai went out from the king dressed in royal clothing of blue and white, "and the city of Shushan rejoiced and was glad. The Jews had light and gladness, joy and honor" (verses 15-16). Everywhere the decree went out, the Jews there rejoiced with a feast and celebration.

The chapter ends with an interesting note: Many people converted to Judaism at this point. When they saw how God worked on behalf of the Jews, they signed up and became Jews. Suddenly it was a lot safer to be a Jew.

One Jewish commentator said that when the Jews saw the miracle of their deliverance, they accepted the Torah with great enthusiasm. Seeing this, the Gentiles gained new respect for the Torah (Genesis through Deuteronomy) and its teaching, and they converted as well. This could be called an Old Testament revival because of what God did to deliver His people.

Application

The Power of God to Reverse the Irreversible

Sometimes we are told concerning the condition of a sick person, "There is no hope." While it may be true from human experience or a medical perspective that there is no hope, the only One who can really say there is no hope is the God of hope. God can reverse the irreversible. One of the things you can always hold out to people is the hope of Almighty God who can turn things around. There may be no way to turn a situation around, but there is a God in heaven who can do it.

The Power of the Gospel to Overrule the Power of Sin

There are two decrees in the book of Esther: the decree of death and the decree of life. One of the things we learn in studying the Bible is that God has a way to save sinners. You can't go to heaven by your own good works. You can never be good enough to go to heaven. The Bible says, "You must be born again" (John 3:7). The reason you must be born again is that a decree has been written that the wages of sin is death. The decree has been written that no one can go to heaven with his sin.

God will not overturn that decree. We violate God the day we are born because of our own sin that we inherited. But the good news is that, just as the decree in Persia was overruled by another decree, God has given us another decree. That decree is that if we believe on the Lord Jesus Christ, we will be saved.

When the people of Israel murmured against God, He sent serpents among them. Those snakes began to bite the Israelites, and the Israelites died from the venom. God didn't go into the camp and say, "I'm going to change my mind about that. I'm going to make it so that from now on, when they bite, it won't be the sting of death." God didn't do that. He had already declared the decree of death. Instead, God raised up a pole and put a serpent on the pole. Then He said, "Here's decree number two. Look and live!" If you will look at that pole, representing salvation, then the sting of the sin will be overruled.

There is redemption everywhere in the Bible—in precept, in illustration, and in teaching.

The Plan of God to Reach the World

When the decree of life was finally written for the Jews in Persia, the courtiers went out on royal steeds, "hastened and pressed on by the king's command. And the decree was issued in Shushan the citadel" (verse 14). When you have a decree of life, you get on the fastest horse you can find and you go as quickly as possible to tell everyone, "The decree of death has been overruled, and now there is a decree of life!" That's what a missionary does. That's what all Christians are supposed to do.

Imagine what it would have been like to have been appointed one of the couriers, given the fastest horse, a destination, and a scroll under your arm. What would it be like to ride off and tell people the curse of their death had been overruled?

Imagine what it would have been like to be a Jew and have a courier come up and say to you, "You don't have to worry about that date of judgment because God has worked out a plan whereby you can live."

Somehow we don't fully believe that the whole world is lost and on its way to hell. If we really believed that, we would get the fastest horse we could find, ride down through the neighborhoods, and say, "There's a new decree that overrules the old one. It is a decree of life. Look and live!"

Too often we lose the sense of urgency in our lives as believers. It's easy to get caught up in the humdrum of trying to meet one crisis after another. It takes so much time to be alive. But there is an urgent message that needs to be circulated. The greatest opportunity we have in this life is to go as messengers of Jesus Christ and tell people there is a law that has been put on the books that overrules the law by which most of them are being judged. Let's find the fastest horse we can and go and tell them.

PERSONAL QUESTIONS

1. Read Esther 8:1-8.

   a. What did the king give to Esther in verse 1?

   b. What did he learn about his queen and her connection to Mordecai? (verse 1)

   c. Mordecai received what from the king and from the queen? (verse 2)

   d. In verse 5 Esther pleads with the king again on behalf of the Jewish people. What four phrases did she set up her request with?

e. What was the king's response to Esther's request? (verses 7-8)

2. Read Esther 8:9-17.

   a. Why did Mordecai and Esther take their time in writing the new decree?

   b. What did the new decree declare the Jews were allowed to do? (verse 11)

c. How was the decree distributed throughout the Persian Empire? (verse 10)

d. When the Jews heard the new decree, how did they react? (verse 17)

3. Describe a time in your life or the life of someone you know when God reversed the irreversible. What did this circumstance teach you about God's power?

GROUP QUESTIONS

1. Read Esther 8:1-8 together.

   a. Discuss why even though Haman was dead, the Jews were still in danger of being killed.

   b. What did Esther request of the king in verses 4-6?

   c. How did the king respond to Esther's request? (verses 7-8)

   d. What was the new decree that Mordecai and Esther wrote? What did it allow the Jewish people to do? (verses 11-12)

e. Describe the reaction of the Jewish people as they heard about the second decree. (verse 17)

2. Share with the group about a time in your life or the life of someone you know when God reversed the irreversible.

3. Discuss how God's power is on display throughout the first eight chapters of Esther.

DID YOU KNOW?

The phrase "became Jews" is found only one time in the Old Testament— in this eighth chapter of the book of Esther. In fact, there are very few times the Old Testament gives evidence of Gentiles becoming Jews. There were some isolated incidents, but in the book of Esther there was a mass conversion. In Esther 8:17, we read: "And in every province and city, wherever the king's command and decree came, the Jews had joy and gladness, a feast and a holiday. Then many of the people of the land became Jews, because fear of the Jews fell upon them."

The Extermination of Enemies

Esther 9:1-16

In this lesson we will see the vengeance of the Jews upon their enemies.

OUTLINE

As we study the retaliation of the Jews, we will learn about the overwhelming power of prejudice and hatred. We will also examine the attitudes of the Bible toward retaliation.

I. **The Reversal of Power**

II. **The Retaliation Against Persecutors**

III. **The Record of the Casualties**

IV. **The Request for Added Revenge**

V. **The Restraint Concerning the Spoil**

VI. **Application**
   A. The Power of Hatred and Prejudice
   B. The Place of Retaliation
   C. The Protection and the Promise of God

OVERVIEW

In a short time, the tables turned on Haman and his henchmen. Mordecai and Esther were now in the power positions. Through the decree of King Xerxes, they were allowed to go back and exact vengeance on those who were going to exterminate the entire Jewish race.

Vengeance and retaliation have been a part of this world as far back as Cain and Abel. In this story of Esther, we have the classic presentation of retaliatory action.

THE REVERSAL OF POWER

On the day the enemies of the Jews hoped to gain mastery over the Jews, the reverse happened. The Jews themselves gained mastery over those who hated them. In one day, the plans of wicked Haman were turned upside down. Instead of the Persians hunting the Jews to annihilate them, the Jews were now hunting the Persian anti-Semites to take away their lives. Mordecai gave the counter decree on June 25, 474 B.C. That decree was carried out on March 7, 473 B.C. The Jews had most of the summer and winter months to get ready for this momentous day, and they were ready.

For a period of time throughout the Persian Empire, it was like a civil war: two opposing parties ready to leap at each other's throats, each with a legal right to kill one another depending upon which decree they were obeying. Ahasuerus (King Xerxes) had allowed a civil war to erupt right under his nose.

THE RETALIATION AGAINST PERSECUTORS

Everyone who was involved in leadership in the Persian government who had before championed the cause of Haman had now, apparently in one day, switched sides. They were now with Mordecai championing the cause of the Jews. The list of the people in verse 3, "all of the officials of the provinces, the satraps, the governors, and all those doing the king's work," is the same list of those to whom Haman's letter was sent and who were to carry out that decree. The leadership under the Persian government had decided it wasn't going to be profitable to continue championing the cause of Haman. Haman was out, Mordecai in.

Haman's letter had truly stirred up the people within the Jewish community. When they were given permission to go after the people who were coming after them, they slayed 75,000 people. Evidently, there were 75,000 people within the Persian Empire who were actively seeking the death of the Jewish community. This was no small conflict. This was a major uprising.

Perhaps one reason the political system so quickly moved to the cause of the Jews was that the leaders may have remembered something that had happened 65 years earlier. At that time, in approximately the same area, Darius the Mede sentenced Daniel to the lions' den. After God preserved Daniel through that ordeal, Darius was so happy that he had the men who had maliciously accused Daniel thrown into the lions' den. These men and their families were killed before they even hit the floor of the den. The leaders in the Persian Empire who served under Xerxes and had been influenced by Haman probably knew this story and figured they had better hurry and get on the side of the Jews. They feared Mordecai because he was getting more and more powerful. It was evident that the power of God was on his life, and there is nothing more intimidating than being around somebody who is under the power of God and to be on the wrong side of the issue. So these people joined with Mordecai and Esther and became a part of the purging of the anti Semitic view within the empire.

The Record of the Casualties

Verse 5 says that the Jewish people did what they pleased. Apparently that means they searched out the leading anti-Semites and did not just wait to defend themselves against them, but rather they took the offensive. They went after the leaders and killed this group in the palace.

In verses 7 through 10 we are told that Haman's ten sons were killed. Some have said this doesn't seem right. The sons had already lost their inheritance. When Haman was killed, everything he owned was given to Esther and Mordecai. All of Haman's sons had nothing. It seems like that would be penalty enough. Now they were not only killed but also hung up in public and desecrated for all to see.

One author wrote that if there were pockets of resistance after the slaying, looking forward to a second round, then Esther's request for the sons' public desecration could be understood as a way to stop further rebellion from the anti-Semites.[1] It's difficult to believe that Haman's sons could have escaped inheriting hatred for the Jews when Haman lived for the day he could destroy the entire Jewish population in Persia.

People were killed in the palace, and Haman's sons were killed. Next the record shows that five hundred people were killed in Shushan the citadel alone. Evidently that many people in the citadel were trying to destroy the Jews. Esther lived in the citadel. The chances of her survival would have been slim if the Jews had not taken the offensive against the anti-Jewish persecutors.

In verses 15 and 16 we are given the total of the casualties: 75,000 people died. Many commentators before the time of Hitler considered that number very unlikely. Then Hitler annihilated with 6 million Jews, plus the people of many other races. Suddenly 75,000 in Persia sounded possible. The Persian Empire at the time of Esther varied in its population from 73 million to 100 million. The Jews probably numbered 2 or 3 million. Of those, about 500,000 could bear arms. These might destroy 75,000 in battle throughout the entire empire.

Ahasuerus didn't grieve over losing nearly a million men. In the Greek war they fought between chapter 1 and chapter 2, he lost a million men. A man like Xerxes used the blood of men to accomplish gain. So the loss of 75,000 anti-Jewish people in the Persian Empire probably didn't faze Xerxes in the least. In fact, he was quite interested to know what was happening and how many people were killed.

The Request for Added Revenge

Xerxes wanted a report on the retaliation. Then he asked, "Now what is your petition? It shall be granted to you. Or what is your further request? It shall be done" (verse 12). In other words, "How many more people do you want killed?" The Jews had already had a field day. It had been open season on all the anti-Semites in the Persian Empire. But when Xerxes asked Esther what more he could do to help, her reply was to ask for one more day to fight their enemies.

So the king gave the Jews in Shushan another day to go after the Persian haters of the Jews. Some have said that this response from Esther doesn't seem to mesh with the gracious, godly spirit that Esther is so often portrayed as having. It wasn't a meek response. But it was effective in saving her people from their enemies.

The Restraint Concerning the Spoil

Sometimes people say this chapter shows unrestrained retaliation on the part of Esther, Mordecai, and the Jews. But there was a measure of restraint even in what Esther and Mordecai did to the 75,000 people who were killed. In the decree against the enemies of the Jews, they were given permission to do three things. They could destroy the men, they could destroy the women and children, and they could take all of the spoil they could gather from these people. But they only did one of the three things, they killed the men.

Although it may have been a literary device that the report of men killed stood for the whole, there is no evidence in the chapter that women or children were destroyed. There is absolute proof positive that they did not take any of that which they were permitted to take by the decree. The only reasonable reason for this was that there was restraint on the part of these people in carrying out the preservation of the Jewish race within the Persian government. The Jews retaliated, but not to the full extent of the law.

Perhaps they remembered what happened with Saul and the Amalekites. Saul lost the kingship because he kept the spoil of the Amalekites. He lied to God about it, and God took away his authority.

Application

The Power of Hatred and Prejudice

In the first two chapters of Esther, there is no evidence of general hatred toward the Jews. There is the hatred of one man for one other man. Haman hated Mordecai because he wouldn't bow down to Haman, second-in-command. Haman's hatred of Mordecai was developed into a hatred of not just one man, but of a whole race known as the Jews. That hatred, which was just barely observable in the heart of one man at the beginning of the book, was fanned into white-hot heat. It developed into hatred of the Jewish people, not just on the part of Haman, but on the part of much of the leadership of Persia. It grew until it became a civil war between the Jews and the Persians. Hatred is a powerful force. It is possible that it was a force inherited by Haman's sons, and that's why they weren't allowed to perpetuate that hatred in the generation to come.

Prejudice and hatred still live, even in the hearts of some of God's people. Here in Esther is a massive picture of what can happen when hatred is allowed to develop in the heart of one man, and then to envelop an entire nation. Hatred left unchecked is a malignant cancer that ends by destroying everything it touches.

The Place of Retaliation

There seem to be four levels of retaliation in the Bible. The first could be called "unlimited retaliation." That's what is present in the Old Testament before the giving of the law. In the days before the law there were no restraints on vengeance. In Genesis 4:23-24, Lamech is recorded as saying, "I have killed a man for wounding me, even a young man for hurting me. If Cain shall be avenged sevenfold, then Lamech seventy-sevenfold."

When the law was given, retaliation moved to the second level—what could be called "limited retaliation." Under Mosaic Law, retaliation was limited to the actual loss suffered. The model for retaliation in Exodus 21:24 was that if an eye was lost, then the retaliation would also be an eye. You could only retaliate in keeping with the damage that had been done to you.

In the New Testament, there is a third level concerning retaliation that could be called "no retaliation." Vengeance belongs to the Lord. The person offended simply refrains from retaliating. That's always to be at least what the Christian is to do. We are never allowed vengeance or retaliation against another Christian. We can allow the law to take its course in the hearts of people who have offended the law, but as individuals, we are not allowed to retaliate against another.

Finally, there is a fourth level that goes even beyond this. This one may be called "replaced retaliation." This is the way Jesus taught us to treat our enemies. In this level, you do not retaliate against the enemy, you get rid of the enemy. You destroy the enemy by making him your friend. He can't be your friend and enemy all at once. So you replace retaliation with praying for him and doing good to him. Hopefully in the process, he ceases to be your enemy and becomes your friend. This is how we are to handle retaliation in this generation.

The Protection and the Promise of God

The preservation of the Jewish nation is the most miraculous story you will ever read about apart from your redemption. God constantly seems to bring the Jews to the precipice of extermination, and at the right moment, God comes through and preserves the nation. From its birth in Abraham and down through Jesus and into the future, God has promised that He has a plan for His people.

We have a marvelous God who keeps promises. The book of Esther is just another illustration.

Note

1. John C. Whitcomb, *Esther: The Triumph of God's Sovereignty* (Chicago, IL: Moody Press, 1979), 115.

PERSONAL QUESTIONS

1. Read Esther 9:1-16.

   a. What happened on the day that the enemies of the Jews planned to kill them? (verse 1)

   b. How many people were killed in Shushan? (verses 6, 15) In the rest of the Persian Empire? (verse 16)

   c. What happened to Haman's sons? (verse 7-8, 13-14)

2. According to the decree, what three things were the Jewish people given permission to do to their enemies?

a. Of those three things, which of them did they do and which did they not do?

b. Why might they have exercised restraint against their enemies?

3. Review the section in the lesson titled "The Place of Retaliation."

   a. What was the initial rule about retaliation before the law was given? (Genesis 4:23-24)

   b. Under the Mosaic Law, what was the rule about retaliation? (Exodus 21:24)

c. According to the New Testament, what is the third level of retaliation?

d. Describe the fourth level of retaliation, also found in the New Testament.

e. What level of retaliation do you regularly choose when someone hurts you?

f. What are some practical ways you can implement the fourth level of retaliation when someone hurts you?

GROUP QUESTIONS

1. Read Esther 9:1-16 as a group.

   a. Discuss what occurred in the Persian Empire on the thirteenth day of Adar.

   b. Why might the government officials have switched to Mordecai's side in relation to the decree against the Jewish people?

   c. What request did Esther make of the king in verse 13?

   d. What was the result of her request? (verses 14-15)

e. In what ways did the Jewish people exercise restraint against their enemies? (verse 16)

2. List and discuss the four levels of retaliation that are found in Scripture.

•

•

•

•

3. Think back over the entire book of Esther and make a list of the people and events that God used to lead to the protection of His people.

4. How has God used people and events to protect you in your life? If comfortable, share with the group a specific example of God's protection of you.

DID YOU KNOW?

When Benjamin Franklin was our ambassador to the court of France, he was invited to appear before an atheistic society and present a paper. He took to that society a copy of the book of Esther, which he had transcribed from the Bible, and read it to those present. They were loud in their praise of the paper and said it was one of the most beautiful stories they had ever heard. They asked him where he had secured it. When he told them he had taken it out of the Bible, they dismissed the story, and they dismissed Benjamin Franklin.

The Feast of Purim

Esther 9:17–10:3

In this lesson we will be reminded that we have a sovereign God who is in control.

OUTLINE

As we study the celebration of the victorious Jews, we will learn that our God is a celebratory God and that He continues to care for His people today as He cared for His people during that time of potential annihilation.

I. The Designation of Jewish Feasts

II. The Description of the Feast of Purim

III. The Dates of the Feast of Purim

IV. The Details of the Feast of Purim

V. Application: What Is Apparent and What Is Real

OVERVIEW

The book of Esther is a classic illustration of the anti-Semitism that has been a part of Jewish history since its very beginning. Studying this book, we have learned that anti-Semitism is a path that always leads to destruction, not of the Jews, but of the perpetrators.

THE DESIGNATION OF JEWISH FEASTS

The only thing left after the anti-Semites finish their work is a new feast of celebration for the Jews. When Pharaoh let the Israelites go, they had Passover and still celebrate it every year. After Antiochus Epiphanes, they had Hanukkah and celebrate it around Christmastime every year. When Hitler lost the war, Israel was recognized as a nation in 1948 and now celebrates their independence each year. When Haman's treacherous act was foiled, a brand-new feast was inaugurated by the Jews called the Feast of Purim.

The Feast of Purim has to be understood in the significant history of the book of Esther. Anti-Semitism is based on the hatred of one group of people for the Jews. The key anti-Semite in the book of Esther was Haman. He hated Mordecai for not bowing down to him, and he transferred his hatred to include the whole of Mordecai's people, the Jews. His plan was to annihilate them.

But what happened was that he and his sons and all those who were going to annihilate the Jews with him were destroyed instead. The physical salvation of the Jews had been wrought. Now it was time to celebrate.

THE DESCRIPTION OF THE FEAST OF PURIM

Sometimes we picture God as austere. We think He is not interested in joy and happiness. When we get to heaven, that idea will be forgotten. We are going to have one grand and glorious celebration. The Feast of Purim is a picture of celebration.

The day after the Jews had retaliated on their enemies, they rested and made that day one of feasting and gladness, except for the Jews in Shushan who had an extra day of retaliation before they rested and feasted. Verse 19 says, "Therefore the Jews of the villages who dwelt in the unwalled towns celebrated the fourteenth day of the month of Adar with gladness and feasting, as a holiday, and for sending presents to one another."

Mordecai wrote about this celebration and sent letters to the Jews throughout all the provinces to establish this custom of feasting, this observation "as the days on which the Jews had rest from their enemies, as the month which was turned from sorrow to joy for them, and from mourning to a holiday; that they should make them days of feasting and joy, of sending presents to one another and gifts to the poor" (verse 22). This was the month it all got turned around. Instead of being the victims, they were the victors. Instead of being the conquered, they were the conquerors. Instead of being annihilated, they were liberated.

Verses 27 and 28 say, "The Jews established and imposed it upon themselves and their descendants and all who would join them, that without fail they should celebrate these two days every year, according to the written instructions and according to the prescribed time, that these days should be remembered and kept throughout every generation, every family, every province, and every city, that these days of Purim should not fail to be observed among the Jews, and that the memory of them should not perish among their descendants."

The name of the feast came from the time when Haman cast lots, or *pur*, to determine that day when the Jews would be destroyed. The Feast of Purim is the reminder of the time lots were cast to destroy the Jews, and the lot was turned back on the destroyer. The lots that were thrown for Israel's destruction ended up deciding the very time at which the new national celebration was set because they had been victorious.

Sometimes the Feast of Purim is known as the Feast of Esther. A non-canonical book, 2 Maccabees, refers to it as Mordecai's Day. Purim commemorates the deliverance of God's people at the hands of Esther and Mordecai.

The Dates of the Feast of Purim

The Feast of Purim is the last feast of the year on the Jewish calendar. There it occurs on the fourteenth day of Adar, which corresponds to late February or early March. It is one month to the day before the Feast of Passover. In Jerusalem today, Purim is celebrated on Adar 15, one day later than the rest of the world. This commemorates the fact that the Jews in Ancient Persia in Shushan the palace did not rest from fighting their enemies until the following day. This is known in Israel today as Shushan Purim, reminding them of the extra work that was done by the Jews at that time.

Sometimes today the feast is preceded by a fast day to commemorate the three days of fasting by the Jews' petitioning the king. So sometimes today, the Jews in preparation for the Feast of Purim, go through a time of fasting.

The Details of the Feast of Purim

The most prominent feature during the feast is the reading of the scroll of Esther. The Jews have a handwritten scroll of the book of Esther which they read in the evening service and then again the next day during the morning synagogue service. The book of Esther is known as the *megalah,* "the scroll" in Hebrew. It is the best known of the five books of the Hebrew Bible known as the scrolls. These scrolls are short, and each of the scrolls is read on a different holiday. The Song of Solomon is read at the Feast of Passover. The book of Ruth is read on the Feast of Weeks. The book of Ecclesiastes is read on the Feast of Tabernacles. And, of course, Esther is read on the Feast of Purim.

During Purim, the divine command to blot out the name of Amalek is taken literally. When Haman's name is read from the scroll of Esther, it is met with a thunderous roar of clapping from the Jewish people. They not only clap, they stamp their feet and boo and make a grinding noise with special noisemakers called "graggers."

During the celebration some Jews write Haman's name on the bottoms of their shoes. As they stamp their feet during the reading of the scroll, Haman's name is literally erased off the bottom of their shoes.

Another tradition was known as beating Haman. It involved building an effigy of Haman, which was then hung and burned. This tradition was abandoned during the Middle Ages when anti-Semitic slanders were leveled at the Jewish people that they were burning a figure of Jesus on the cross.

Before the reading of the scroll, it is customary to pass a plate in the synagogue in remembrance of the ancient time when each of the Israelite males brought one half shekel for the maintenance of the temple. Each worshiper places a gift of silver coins, such as a silver dollar or half dollar, on the plate. The donor then "owns" all the money and picks up the coins on the plate, but then immediately donates back to the plate, fulfilling the ancient command. The collection is usually given to help the poor because part of the celebration is giving gifts to the poor.

They also send "presents to one another and gifts to the poor" (verse 22). They take portions of food and delicacies to friends. This Purim tradition is continued even today. The outward expression of joy involves sending a plate full of pastries or cake or fruit and nuts by the hand of a child to friends and relatives. It is customary to give gifts to at least two poor persons during Purim so they can enjoy the festival. What a marvelous way to celebrate—not only to consider your own joy, but also to look around for others who may not have anything to enjoy and give to them.

Purim is a time of special holiday foods. The most popular of these is *hamantaschen*. These are delicious triangular pastries filled with poppyseeds or prune filling. Their name is derived from two German words, *mon*, which is "poppyseed," and *taschen*, which is "pockets." According to tradition, *hamantaschen* are often served for breakfast on the day of the Feast of Purim.

Another festive dish the Jews eat is *kreplach*. *Kreplach* are noodle-like triangular pieces of dough that are stuffed with chopped meat and minced onion filling and served in a thick steaming soup. Eating these special holiday foods is a celebration of a time of gladness. Purim is one of the happiest holidays in the Jewish calendar because it was a time when God overturned the enemies of the Jews and gave victory to His people.

Application: What Is Apparent and What Is Real

We live in a world where apparently we are often defeated. But we know that in reality, we are the victors. We live in a world where often we appear to be the underdogs. But we know because we have read the end of the story that we are the "upperdogs." We are God's people. We are kings and priests of His Kingdom.

The book of Esther is permeated with irony. Haman built the gallows for Mordecai, but Haman himself was hanged on those gallows. Haman was trying to solidify his position in the kingdom, but his position was given instead to Mordecai. Haman tried to kill Mordecai's people, but he and all ten of his sons and all those who hated the Jews were killed instead. Haman tried to wipe out the worship of the true God which prevented men from bowing to him, but instead many of the people of the land became Jews, "because fear of the Jews fell upon them" (Esther 8:17).

Going through the book of Esther, it is uncanny what irony there is in what was apparent and what was real. Sometimes when we look at what is going on in the world, it seems quite apparent that something is very wrong. But that's not real. What's real is that God is on His throne. What's real is that He is in control. What's real is that, while we can't always understand what He is up to, we are going to win. We are victors and conquerors in Jesus Christ.

The exciting thing for the Jewish people is that one day there is going to be deliverance for them that's not just out of danger to their physical lives. There is coming a time when all Israel shall be saved. One of the verses the people of Israel read from the Old Testament during the Feast of Purim is a verse that talks about their ultimate deliverance. It actually has in it the Hebrew word *Immanuel*, which is the word for Jesus, "God with us." The salvation of the Jews will one day be accomplished in completeness even as it is being completely accomplished in the lives of many people today.

We have a wonderful future with our Lord. The book of Esther is just another reminder that we have a great and sovereign God who is in control. As He cared for His people during the time of potential annihilation, He continues to care for His people today.

PERSONAL QUESTIONS

1. Read Esther 9:17–10:3.
   a. How did the Jewish people celebrate after they killed their enemies?

   b. What feast did Mordecai establish for the Jewish people?

   c. Why did he establish this feast? (verses 27-28)

   d. What did the time of celebration involve?

e. How is Mordecai described in Esther 10?

2. What have you learned about God's sovereignty through this study of the book of Esther?

3. What is the most important truth you have learned from this study, and how can you apply it to your life?

GROUP QUESTIONS

1. Read Esther 9:17-32 together.

   a. Describe how the Jewish people celebrated after defeating their enemies.

   b. According to verse 22, what did Mordecai say the Feast of Purim should include?

2. Discuss the importance of remembering God's work in our life.

3. How do the Jewish feasts, specifically Purim, help them remember God's sovereignty in the life of their nation?

4. Based on the information found in this lesson, discuss what the Feast of Purim includes today.

5. Share with the group what you have learned about God's sovereignty through studying the book of Esther.

6. If comfortable, share how God has used this study to help you grow closer to Him.

DID YOU KNOW?

Antiochus Epiphanes lived between the times of the Old and New Testaments. He was literally known as Antiochus the Madman. He did horrible things to the Jews: killing pigs and spattering blood all over the synagogues, taking portions of the animal and stuffing it down the throats of the Jewish priests and rabbis, and taking a pig into the holy of holies in the temple and sacrificing it on the Jewish altar. He killed many Jews during the intertestamental period. After these episodes ended, Hanukkah was established.

ADDITIONAL RESOURCES
by Dr. David Jeremiah

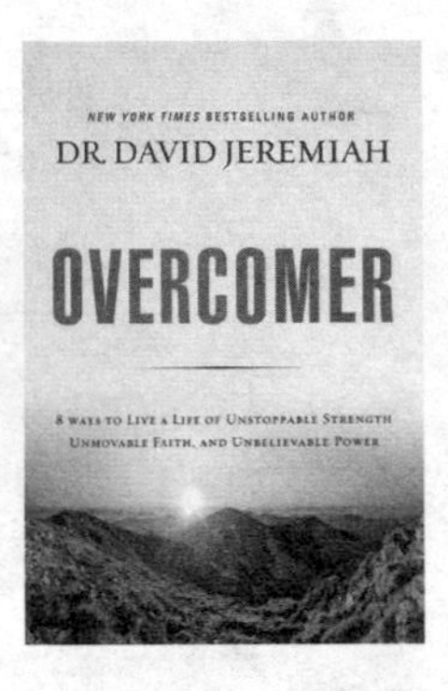

Overcomer

The idea of "overcoming" has transformed over time. When Christ came, the battlefield changed from plains and fields to the human mind and heart. In the *Overcomer* book, Dr. Jeremiah uses Paul's description of spiritual armor to teach us how we are called to overcome in this world of sin, explaining how, when we "put on" Christ, we can stand firm against the evil one.

Slaying the Giants in Your Life

Which giant is intimidating you? Perhaps it is fear or loneliness. Whichever giant is bullying you, the message of *Slaying the Giants in Your Life* is that God has the strength to bring you victory! You never walk alone and never have to live defeated. In this book Dr. Jeremiah will help you to recognize these truths and use them to banish the giants from the promised land of your life.